Service Operation based on ITIL® V

Other publications by Van Haren Publishing

Van Haren Publishing (VHP) specializes in titles on Best Practices, methods and standards within IT management, Architecture (Enterprise and IT), business management and project management.

These publications are grouped in series, eg: *ITSM Library* (on behalf of ITSMF International), *Best Practice* and *IT Management Topics*. VHP is also publisher on behalf of leading companies and institutions, eg The Open Group, IPMA-NL, CA, Getronics, Pink Elephant. At the time of going to press the following books are available:

IT (Service) Management / IT Governance

ITSM, ITIL® V3 and ITIL® V2
Foundations of IT Service Management – based on ITIL® V3 (English, Dutch, German; French, Japanese and Spanish editions)
Introduction to IT Service Management (ITIL V3, English)
IT Service Management based on ITIL V3 – A Pocket Guide (English, Dutch, German, Italian; French, Japanese and Spanish editions)
Foundations of IT Service Management based on ITIL® (ITIL V2), (English, Dutch, French, German, Spanish, Japanese, Chinese, Danish, Italian, Korean, Russian, Arabic; also available as a CD-ROM)
Implementing Service and Support Management Processes (English)
Release and Control for IT Service Management, based on ITIL® – A Practitioner Guide (English)

ISO/IEC 20000
ISO/IEC 20000 – An Introduction (English, German)
Implementing ISO/IEC 20000 Certification (English)
ISO/IEC 20000 – A Pocket Guide (English, Italian, German, Spanish, Portuguese)

ISO 27001 and ISO 17799
Information Security based on ISO 27001 and ISO 17799 – A Management Guide (English)
Implementing Information Security based on ISO 27001 and ISO 17799 – A Management Guide (English)

COBIT
IT Governance based on COBIT4.1® – A Management Guide (English, German, Japanese)

IT Service CMM
IT Service CMM – A Pocket Guide (English)

ASL and BiSL
ASL – A Framework for Application Management (English, German)
ASL – Application Services Library – A Management Guide (English, Dutch)
BiSL – A Framework for Business Information Management (Dutch, English)
BiSL – Business information Services Library – A Management Guide (Dutch; English)

ISPL
IT Services Procurement op basis van ISPL (Dutch)
IT Services Procurement based on ISPL – A Pocket Guide (English)

Other IT Management titles:
De RfP voor IT-outsourcing (Dutch; English version due Spring 2008)
Decision- en Controlfactoren voor IT-Sourcing (Dutch)
Defining IT Success through the Service Catalogue (English)
Frameworks for IT Management – An introduction (English, Japanese; German)
Frameworks for IT Management – A Pocket Guide (English, German, Dutch)
Implementing IT Governance (English)
Implementing leading standards for IT management (English, Dutch)
IT Service Management global best practices, volume 1 (English)
IT Service Management Best Practices, volume 1, 2, 3 and 4 (Dutch)
ITSM from hell! / ITSM from hell based on Not ITIL (English)
ITSMP – The IT Strategy Management Process (English)

Metrics for IT Service Management (English, Russian)
Service Management Process Maps (English)
Six Sigma for IT Management (English)
Six Sigma for IT Management – A Pocket Guide (English)

MOF/MSF
MOF – Microsoft Operations Framework, A Pocket Guide (Dutch, English, French, German, Japanese)
MSF – Microsoft Solutions Framework, A Pocket Guide (English, German)

Architecture (Enterprise and IT)

TOGAF, The Open Group Architecture Framework – A Management Guide (English)
The Open Group Architecture Framework – 2007 Edition (English, official publication of TOG)
TOGAF™ Version 8 Enterprise Edition – Study Guide (English, official publication of TOG)
TOGAF™ Version 8.1.1 Enterprise Edition –A Pocket Guide (English, official publication of TOG)

Business Management

ISO 9000
ISO 9001:2000 – The Quality Management Process (English)

EFQM
The EFQM excellence model for Assessing Organizational Performance – A Management Guide (English)

SqEME®
Process management based on SqEME® (English)
SqEME® – A Pocket Guide (English, Dutch)

Project/Programme/Risk Management

ICB/NCB
NCB Versie 3– Nederlandse Competence Baseline (Dutch, on behalf of IPMA-NL)
Projectmanagement op basis van NCB V3 – IPMA-C en IPMA-D (Dutch)

PRINCE2™
Project Management based on PRINCE2™– Edition 2005 (English, Dutch, German)
PRINCE2™ – A No Nonsense Management Guide (English)
PRINCE2™ voor opdrachtgevers – Management Guide (Dutch)

MINCE®
MINCE® – A Framework for Organizational Maturity (English)

MSP
Programme Management based on MSP (English, Dutch)
Programme Management based on MSP – A Management Guide (English)

M_o_R
Risk Management based on M_o_R – A Management Guide (English)

Other publications on project management:
Wegwijzer voor methoden bij Projectvolwassenheid (Dutch: fall 2008)
Het Project Management Office – Management Guide (Dutch)

For the latest information on VHP publications, visit our website: www.vanharen.net

Service Operation
based on ITIL® V3

A Management Guide

Van Haren
PUBLISHING

Colophon

Title: Service Operation based on ITIL V3® - A Management Guide

Authors: Jan van Bon (Chief Editor, Inform-IT)
                    Arjen de Jong (co-author, Inform-IT)
                    Axel Kolthof (co-author, Inform-IT)
                    Mike Pieper (co-author, Inform-IT)
                    Ruby Tjassing (co-author, Inform-IT)
                    Annelies van der Veen (co-author, Inform-IT)
                    Tieneke Verheijen (co-author, Inform-IT)

Copy editor: Jayne Wilkinson

Publisher: Van Haren Publishing, Zaltbommel, www.vanharen.net

Design & layout: CO2 Premedia bv, Amersfoort - NL

ISBN: 9789087531270

Edition: First edition, first impression, June 2008

Foreword

ITIL receives more and more attention on a global scale, with many companies adopting its principles. In that respect, ITIL version 2 has done a good job. The update of ITIL in version 3, released in June 2007, has caused some concern for many of these companies, since it built on the idea that companies had already achieved results with version 2 content. In practice however, most companies are still working their way through the basic principles of ITIL. For that reason, the "Foundations of IT Service Management - based on ITIL V3" was developed, offering a comprehensive but easy-to-understand source of information on ITIL. This title is now widely used as the authoritative guide on ITIL V3 in training situations and in implementations.

Apart from offering the market a summarized, easy-to-understand source on ITIL V3, that can be used for a step-by-step approach, many companies focus on a subset of the ITIL best practices. That is why we developed a series of ITIL Management Guides, focusing on the processes, procedures, and functions, from each of the phases of the ITIL V3 Lifecycle. This enables companies to focus on those phases that are of primary concern to them.

Each of the five ITIL V3 Management Guides is structured the same way as the successful Foundations book: it separates the Lifecycle information from the single process, procedure and function components, enabling organizations to take their own approach and still adopt ITIL best practices.

The content of each guide was derived from the Foundations book, which ensures that you'll find the same high quality as usual. This means that all content has been peer-reviewed in a rigorous way, making sure that it completely aligns to ITIL V3, but also that it was the best, concise and comprehensive summary of ITIL V3 core content that could be achieved.

I'm convinced that this new management guide will provide an excellent reference tool for practitioners, students and others who want to have a practical guide on the key ITIL V3 concepts.

Jan van Bon
Chief Editor

Acknowledgements

This Management Guide is a compilation of the itSMF publication "Foundations of IT Service Management - Based on ITIL V3". Thus, the international review team that reviewed "Foundations of IT Service Management", has contributed indirectly to this Management Guide. We would like to thank all reviewers once again for their detailed review which improved the quality of both books significantly.

The review team consists of:
- John van Beem, ISES International, Netherlands
- Aad Brinkman, Apreton, Netherlands
- Peter Brooks, PHMB Consulting, itSMF South Africa
- Rob van der Burg, Microsoft, Netherlands
- Judith Cremers, Getronics PinkRoccade Educational Services, Netherlands
- Robert Falkowitz, Concentric Circle Consulting, itSMF Switzerland
- Rosario Fondacaro, Quint Wellington Redwood, Italy
- Peter van Gijn, LogicaCMG, Netherlands
- Jan Heunks, ICT Partners, Netherlands
- Linh Ho, Compuware Corporation, USA
- Ton van der Hoogen, ToTZ Diensten, Netherlands
- Kevin Holland, NHS, UK
- Matiss Horodishtiano, Amdocs, itSMF Israel
- Wim Hoving, BHVB, Netherlands
- Brian Johnson, CA, USA
- Georges Kemmerling, Quint Wellington Redwood, Netherlands
- Kirstie Magowan, itSMF New Zealand
- Steve Mann, OpSys - SM2, itSMF Belgium
- Reiko Morita, Ability InterBusiness Solutions, Inc., Japan
- Jürgen Müller, Marval Benelux, Netherlands
- Ingrid Ouwerkerk, Getronics PinkRoccade Educational Services, Netherlands
- Ton Sleutjes, CapGemini, Netherlands
- Maxime Sottini, Innovative Consulting, itSMF Italy
- Takashi Yagi, Hitachi Ltd., itSMF Japan

Given the desire for a broad consensus in the IT Service Management field, new developments, additional material and contributions from ITSM professionals who have worked with ITIL version 3 are welcome. They will be discussed by the editors and where appropriate incorporated into new editions. Comments can be sent to the Chief Editor, Jan van Bon, email: j.van.bon@inform-it.org.

Contents

x

CHAPTER 1

Introduction

1.1 Background

Developments in IT have had a tremendous effect on the business market during the last decade. Since the appearance of extremely powerful hardware, highly versatile software and super-fast networks, all connected to each other worldwide, organizations have been able to develop their information-dependent products and services to a greater extent, and to bring them to the market much faster. These developments have marked the transition of the industrial age into the **information age**. In the information age, everything has become faster and more dynamic, and everything is connected.

Traditional hierarchical organizations often have difficulties in responding to this rapidly changing market, and this has led to current trends for organizations to become flatter and more flexible. The focus has shifted from vertical silos to horizontal **processes**, and decision-making powers are increasingly bestowed on the employees. It is against this background that the work processes of IT service management have arisen.

An important advantage of process-oriented organizations is that processes can be designed to support a **customer-oriented approach**. This has made the alignment between the IT organization (responsible for supplying information) and the customer (responsible for using these information systems in their business) increasingly significant. Over the last couple of years, this trend has attracted attention under the title of **Business-IT Alignment (BITA)**.

As organizations gained more experience with the **process-oriented approach** of IT service management, it became clear that the process must be managed coherently.

Furthermore, it was obvious that the introduction of a process-oriented work method meant a big change for the primarily line and project-oriented organizations. Culture and change management proved to be crucial elements for a successful organizational design.

Another important lesson learned was that the IT organization must not lose itself in a process culture. Just like the one-sided project-oriented organization, a one-sided process-oriented organization was not the optimum type of business. Balance was, as always, the magic word. In addition, it became clear that the customer-oriented approach required that an **end-to-end** and **user-centric** approach must be followed: it was of no help to the user to know that "the server was still in operation" if the information system was not available at the user's workplace. IT services must be viewed in a larger context. The need for the recognition of the **Service Lifecycle**, and the management of IT services in light of that lifecycle, became a concern.

Due to the fast growing dependency of business upon information, the quality of information services in companies is being increasingly subjected to stricter **internal and external requirements**. The role of **standards** is getting more and more important, and **frameworks** of "best practices" help with the development of a management system to meet these requirements. Organizations that are not in control of their processes, will not be able to realize great results on the level of the Service Lifecycle and the end-to-end-management of those services. Organizations that do not have their internal organization in order, will also not achieve great results. For these reasons, all these aspects are handled alongside each other in the course of this book.

1.2 Why this book

This book offers detailed information for those who are responsible for strategic information issues, as well as for the (much larger) group who are responsible for setting up and executing the delivery of the information systems. This is supported by both the description of the Service Lifecycle, as documented in ITIL version 3, and by the description of the processes that are associated with it. The ITIL core books are very extensive, and can be used for a thorough study of contemporary best practices. This management guide provides the reader with an easy-to-read comprehensive introduction to the broad library of ITIL core books, to support the understanding and the further distribution of ITIL as an industry standard. Once this understanding of the structure of ITIL has been gained, the reader can use the core books for a more detailed understanding and guidance for their daily practice.

1.3 Organizations

Several organizations are involved in the maintenance of ITIL as a description of the "best practice" in the IT service management field.

OGC

Initially ITIL was a product of the CCTA, a UK Government Organization. On 1 April 2001 the CCTA was incorporated into the OGC, which thus became the new owner of ITIL. The aim of the OGC is to help its clients (within the UK Government) with the modernization of their procurement activities and the improvement of their services, by, among other things, making the best possible use of IT: "OGC aims to modernize procurement in government, and deliver substantial value for money improvements". The OGC promotes the use of "best practices" in numerous areas, such as project management, program management, procurement, risk management and IT service management. For this reason the OGC itself has published several series of books (Libraries) which have been written by (international) experts from different companies and organizations.

itSMF

The target group for this publication is anyone who is involved or interested in IT service management. A professional organization, working on the development of the IT service management field, has been created especially for this target group.

In 1991 the Information Technology Service Management Forum (itSMF), originally known as the Information Technology Infrastructure Management Forum (ITIMF), was set up as a UK association. In 1994, a sister-association was established in the Netherlands, following the UK example.

Since then, independent itSMF organizations have been set up in more than forty countries, spread across the globe, and the number of "chapters" continues to grow. All itSMF organizations operate under the umbrella organization, itSMF International (itSMF-I).

itSMF is aimed at the entire professional area of IT service management. It promotes the exchange of information and experiences that IT organizations can use to improve their service provision. itSMF is also involved in the use and quality of the various standards and methods that are important in the field. One of these standards is ITIL. itSMF International has an agreement with OGC and APM Group on the promotion of the use of ITIL.

APM Group

In 2006, OGC contracted the management of ITIL rights, the certification of ITIL exams and accreditation of training organizations to the APM Group (APMG), a commercial organization. APMG defines the certification and accreditation for the ITIL exams, and published the new certification system (see Section 2.1: ITIL exams).

Exam bodies

The Dutch foundation Examen Instituut voor Informatica (EXIN) and the English Information Systems Examination Board (ISEB, part of the BCS: the British Computer Society) cooperated in the development and provision of certification for IT service management. For many years they were the only bodies that provided ITIL exams. With the contracting of APMG by OGC, the responsibility for ITIL exams is now with APMG. To support the world-wide delivery of these ITIL exams, APMG has accredited a number of exam bodies: EXIN, BCS/ISEB, and Loyalist College, Canada.

1.4   Structure of the book

Chapter 2, introduces the Service Lifecycle, in the context of IT service management and IT governance. It discusses principles of organizational maturity, and the benefits and risks of following a service management framework. This chapter ends with the introduction of the Service Lifecycle.

In Chapters 3 the Service Operation lifecycle phase is discussed in detail, in a standardized structure.

Chapter 4 provides general information on principles of processes, teams, roles, functions, positions, tools, and other elements of interest.

In chapter 5, the processes and functions of Service Operation are described in detail. Each of these processes and functions is described in terms of:
- Introduction
- Activities, methods and techniques
- Interfaces, inputs and outputs
- Metrics and Key Performance Indicators (KPIs)
- Implementation, with Critical Success Factors (CSFs), challenges, risks and traps

The appendices provide useful sources for the reader. A reference list of used sources is provided, as well as the official ITIL Glossary and a list with acronyms. The book ends with an extensive index of relevant terms that will support the reader in finding relevant text elements.

CHAPTER 2

Introduction to the Service Lifecycle

2.1 Introduction to ITIL

In the 1980s the quality of service provided by both internal and external IT companies to UK government departments was of such a level that the CCTA (Central Computer and Telecommunications Agency, now the Office of Government Commerce, OGC) was instructed by the Government to develop a standard approach for an efficient and effective delivery of IT services. This was to be an approach which was independent of the suppliers (whether internal or external). The result of this instruction was the development and publication of the **Information Technology Infrastructure Library™** (ITIL). ITIL is made up of a collection of "best practices " found across the range of IT service providers.

ITIL offers a systematic approach to the delivery of quality of IT services. It gives a detailed description of most of the important processes in an IT organization, and includes checklists for tasks, procedures and responsibilities which can be used as a basis for tailoring to the needs of individual organizations.

At the same time, the broad coverage of ITIL also provides a helpful reference guide for many areas, which can be used to develop new improvement goals for an IT organization, enabling it to grow and mature.

Over the years, ITIL has become much more than a series of useful books about IT service management. The framework for the "best practice" in IT service management is promoted and further developed by advisors, trainers and suppliers of technologies or products. Since the nineties, ITIL represents not only the theoretical framework, but the approach and philosophy shared by the people who work with it in practice.

Being an extended framework of best practices for IT service management itself, the advantages and disadvantages of frameworks in general, described in Section 2.5, are also applicable to ITIL. Of course, ITIL was developed because of the advantages mentioned earlier. Many of the pointers from "best practices" are intended to avoid potential problems, or, should they occur after all, to solve them.

ITIL exams
In 2007 the APM Group launched a new certification scheme for ITIL, based on ITIL version 3. ITIL version 2 will be maintained for a transition period, continuing until the year 2008. **ITIL version 2** has qualifications on three levels:
- **Foundation** Certificate in IT Service Management
- **Practitioner** Certificate in IT Service Management
- **Manager** Certificate in IT Service Management

Until 2000, some 60,000 ITIL certificates had been distributed and by 2006 the number had reached 500,000 certificates.

For **ITIL version 3** a new system of qualifications has been set up. There are four qualification levels:
- Foundation Level
- Intermediate Level (Lifecycle Stream & Capability Stream)
- ITIL Diploma
- Advanced Service Management Professional Diploma

For more information about the ITIL V3 Qualification Scheme, see http://www.itil-officialsite.com/Qualifications/ITILV3QualificationScheme.asp.

2.2   IT governance
With the growing role of information, information systems and IT service management, the management requirements for IT grew as well. These requirements focus on two aspects: the compliance with internal and external policies, laws and regulations, and the provision of added value to the stakeholders of the organization. IT governance is still a very young discipline, with no more than a few acknowledged standards or frameworks available. In contrast, there are many different definitions of IT governance available. A definition that receives a lot of support is the one by Van Grembergen:

> *IT governance* consists of a comprehensive framework of structures, processes and relational mechanisms. Structures involve the existence of responsible functions such as IT executives and accounts, and a diversity of IT Committees. Processes refer to strategic IT decision-making and monitoring. Relational mechanisms include business/IT participation and partnerships, strategic dialogue and shared learning.

There is a clear distinction between governance and management, suggesting that governance enables the creation of a setting in which others can manage their tasks effectively (Sohal & Fitzpatrick). So IT governance and IT management are two separate entities. IT service management can be considered to be part of the IT management domain, which leaves IT governance in the business or information management domain.

Although many frameworks are characterized as "IT Governance frameworks", such as COBIT and even ITIL, most of them are in fact management frameworks. There is at least one standard for IT Governance available: the local Australian standard for Corporate governance of information and communication technology (AS8015-2005).

2.3 Organizational maturity

From the moment **Richard Nolan** introduced his "staged model" for the application of IT in organizations in 1973, many people have used stepwise improvement models. These models were quickly recognized as suitable instruments for quality improvement programs, thereby helping organizations to climb up the maturity ladder.

Dozens of variations on the theme can easily be found, ranging from trades such as software development, acquisition, systems engineering, software testing, website development, data warehousing and security engineering, to help desks and knowledge management. Obviously the *kaizen* principle (improvement works best in smaller steps) was one that appealed to many.

After Nolan's staged model in 1973, the most appealing application of this modeling was found when the Software Engineering Institute (SEI) of Carnegie Mellon University, USA, published its Software Capability Maturity Model (SW-CMM). The CMM was copied and applied in most of the cases mentioned above, making CMM something of a standard in maturity modeling. The CMM was later followed by newer editions, including CMMI (CMM Integration).

Later, these models were applied in quality management models, like the European Foundation for Quality Management (EFQM). Apart from the broad quality management models, there are several other industry accepted practices, such as Six Sigma and Total Quality Management (TQM) which are complementary to ITIL.

The available standards, and frameworks of best practice, offer guidance for organizations in achieving "operational excellence" in IT service management. Depending upon their stage of development, organizations tend to require different kinds of guidance.

Maturity model: CMMI

In the IT industry, the process maturity improvement process is best known in the context of the **Capability Maturity Model Integration (CMMI)**. This process improvement method was developed by the Software Engineering Institute (SEI) of Carnegie Mellon University. CMMI provides both a staged and a continuous model. In the continuous representation, improvement is measured using capability levels. Maturity is measured for a particular process across an organization. In the staged representation, improvement is measured using maturity levels, for a set of processes across an organization.

The capability levels in the **CMMI continuous representation** are:
- **incomplete process** - a process that either is not performed or partially performed
- **performed process** - satisfies the specific goals of the process area
- **managed process** - a performed (capability level 1) process that has the basic infrastructure in place to support the process
- **defined process** - a managed (capability level 2) process that is tailored from the organization's set of standard processes according to the organization's tailoring guidelines, and contributes work products, measures and other process improvement information to the organizational process assets
- **quantitatively Managed process** - a defined (capability level 3) process that is controlled using statistical and other quantitative techniques
- **optimizing process** - a quantitatively managed (capability level 4) process that is improved based on an understanding of the common causes of variation inherent in the process

The **CMMI staged representation** model defines five maturity levels, each a layer in the base for the next phase in the ongoing process improvement, designated by the numbers 1 through 5:
1. **initial** - processes are ad hoc and chaotic
2. **managed** - the projects of the organization have ensured that processes are planned and executed in accordance with policy
3. **defined** - processes are well characterized and understood, and are described in standards, procedures, tools and methods

4. **quantitatively managed** - the organization and projects establish quantitative objectives for quality and process performance, and use them as criteria in managing processes
5. **optimizing** - focuses on continually improving process performance through incremental and innovative process and technological improvements

Many other maturity models were based on these structures, such as the Gartner Maturity Models. Most of these models are focused at capability maturity. Some others, like KPMG's World Class IT Maturity Model, take a different approach.

Standard: ISO/IEC 20000

Developing and maintaining a quality system which complies with the requirements of the ISO 9000 (ISO-9000:2000) series can be considered a tool for the organization to reach and maintain the system-focused (or "managed" in IT Service CMM) level of maturity. These ISO standards emphasize the definition, description and design of processes. For IT service management organizations, a specific ISO standard was produced: the ISO/IEC 20000 (see Figure 2.1).

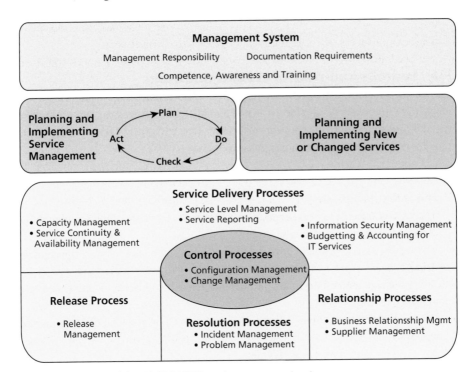

Figure 2.1 Overview of the ISO/IEC 20000 service management system

Customer maturity

When assessing the maturity of an organization, we cannot restrict ourselves to the service provider. The **level of maturity of the customer** (Figure 2.2) is also important. If there are large differences in maturity between the provider and the customer, then these will have to be considered to prevent a mismatch in the approach, methods and mutual expectations. Specifically, this affects the communication between the customer and the provider.

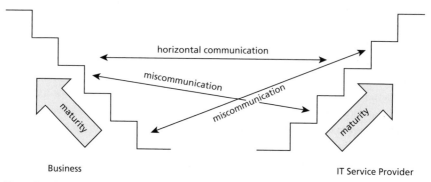

Figure 2.2 Communication and maturity levels: customer and provider

2.4 Benefits and risks of ITSM frameworks

The list below identifies some benefits and possible problems of using IT service management best practices. This list is not intended to be definitive, but is provided here as a basis for considering some of the benefits that can be achieved and some of the mistakes that can be made when using common process-based IT service management frameworks:

Benefits to the customer/user:
- The provision of IT services becomes more customer-focused and agreements about service quality improve the relationship.
- The services are described better, in customer language, and in more appropriate detail.
- Better management of the quality, availability, reliability and cost of the services are managed better.
- Communication with the IT organization is improved by agreeing on the points of contact.

Benefits to the IT organization:

- The IT organization develops a clearer structure, becomes more efficient, and is more focused on the corporate objectives.
- The IT organization is more in control of the infrastructure and services it has responsibility for, and changes become easier to manage.
- An effective process structure provides a framework for the effective outsourcing of elements of the IT services.
- Following best practices encourages a cultural change towards providing service, and supports the introduction of quality management systems based on the ISO 9000 series or on ISO/IEC 20000.
- Frameworks can provide coherent frames of reference for internal communication and communication with suppliers, and for the standardization and identification of procedures.

Potential problems/mistakes:

- The introduction can take a long time and require significant effort, and may require a change of culture in the organization; an overambitious introduction can lead to frustration because the objectives are never met.
- If process structures become an objective in themselves, the service quality may be adversely affected; in this scenario, unnecessary or over-engineered procedures are seen as bureaucratic obstacles, which are to be avoided where possible.
- There is no improvement in IT services due a fundamental lack of understanding about what the relevant processes should provide, what the appropriate performance indicators are, and how processes can be controlled.
- Improvement in the provision of services and cost reductions are insufficiently visible, because no baseline data was available for comparison and/or the wrong targets were identified.
- A successful implementation requires the involvement and commitment of personnel at all levels in the organization; leaving the development of the process structures to a specialist department may isolate that department in the organization and it may set a direction that is not accepted by other departments.
- If there is insufficient investment in appropriate training and support tools, justice will not be done to the processes and the service will not be improved; additional resources and personnel may be needed in the short term if the organization is already overloaded by routine IT service management activities which may not be using "best practices".

2.5   Service Lifecycle: concept and overview

The information provision role and system has grown and changed since the launch of ITIL version 2 (in 2000/02). IT supports and is part of an increasing number of goods and services. In the business world, the information provision role has changed as well: IT's role is no longer just supporting, but has become the baseline for the creation of business value.

ITIL version 3 intends to include and provide insight into IT's new role in all its complexity and dynamics. To that end, a new service management approach has been chosen that does not center around processes, but focuses on the Service Lifecycle.

Basic concepts

Before we describe the Service Lifecycle, we need to define some basic concepts.

Good practice

ITIL is presented as a good practice (literally: correct method). This is an approach or method that has proven itself in practice. These good practices can be a solid backing for organizations that want to improve their IT services. In such cases, the best thing to do is to select a generic standard or method that is accessible to everyone, ITIL, COBIT, CMMI, PRINCE2® and ISO/IEC 20000, for example. One of the benefits of these freely accessible generic standards is that they can be applied to several real-life environments and situations. There is also ample training available for open standards. This makes it much easier to train staff.

Another source for good practice is proprietary knowledge. A disadvantage of this kind of knowledge is that it may be customized for the context and needs of a specific organization. Therefore, it may be difficult to adopt or replicate and it may not be as effective in use.

Service

A service is about creating value for the customer. ITIL defines a service as follows:

> A **service** is a means of delivering value to customers by facilitating outcomes the customers want to achieve without the ownership of specific costs or risks.

Outcomes are possible from the performance of tasks, and they are limited by a number of constraints. Services enhance performance and reduce the pressure of constraints. This increases the chances of the desired outcomes being realized.

Value
Value is the core of the service concept. From the customer's perspective value consists of two core components: utility and warranty. Utility is what the customer receives, and warranty is how it is provided.

Service management
ITIL defines service management as follows:

> **Service management** is a set of specialized organizational capabilities for providing value to customers in the form of services.

ITIL discusses some of the fundamental principles of service management that supplement the functions and processes in the ITIL core books. The next principles may help design a service management system:

- **Specialization & coordination** - The goal of service management is to make capabilities and resources available through services that are useful and acceptable to the customer with regard to quality, costs and risks. The service provider takes the weight of responsibility and resource management off the customer's shoulders so that they can focus on the business' core competence. Service management coordinates the business of service management responsibility with regard to certain resources. *Utility* and *warranty* act as a guide.
- **Agency principle** - Service management always involves an agent and a principal that seconds this agent to fulfill activities on their behalf. Agents may be consultants, advisors or service providers. Service agents act as intermediary between service providers and customers in conjunction with users. Usually, these agents are the service provider's staff, but they can also be self-service systems and processes for users. Value for the customer is created through agreements between principals and agents.
- **Encapsulation** - The customer's interest focuses on the value of use; he prefers to be spared from any technical details and structure complexity. The "encapsulation principle" is focused on hiding what the customer does not need and showing what is valuable and useful to the customer. Three principles are closely linked to this:
  - separation of concerns
  - modularity: a clear, modular structure
  - loose coupling: reciprocal independence of resources and users

Systems
ITIL describes the organizational structure concepts which proceed from system theory. The Service Lifecycle in ITIL version 3 is a system; however, a function, a process or an organization is a system as well. The definition of a system:

> A **system** is a group of interacting, interrelating, or interdependent components that form a unified whole, operating together for a common purpose.

Feedback and learning are two key aspects in the performance of systems; they turn processes, functions and organizations into dynamic systems. Feedback can lead to learning and growth, not only within a process, but also within an organization in its entirety.

Within a process, for instance, the feedback about the performance of one cycle is, in its turn, input for the next process cycle. Within organizations, there can be feedback between processes, functions and lifecycle phases. Behind this feedback is the common goal: the customer's objectives.

Functions and processes
The distinction between functions and processes is important in ITIL.

What is a function?

> A **function** is a subdivision of an organization that is specialized in fulfilling a specified type of work, and is responsible for specific end results.
> Functions are independent subdivisions with capabilities and resources that are required for their performance and results. They have their own practices and their own knowledge body.

What is a process?

> A **process** is a structured set of activities designed to accomplish a defined objective.
> Processes result in a goal-oriented change, and utilize feedback for self-enhancing and self-corrective actions.

Processes possess the following characteristics:
- They are **measurable** because they are performance-oriented.
- They have **specific results**.
- They provide results to **customers** or stakeholders.
- They **respond to a specific event** - a process is indeed continual and iterative, but is always originating from a certain event.

It can be difficult to determine whether something is a function or a process. According to ITIL, whether it is a function or process depends completely on the organizational design. A good example of a function is a service desk, a good example of a process is change management.

The hierarchical structure of functions can lead to the rise of "silos" in which each function is very self-oriented. This does not benefit the success of the organization as a whole. Processes run through the hierarchical structure of functions; functions often share some processes. This is how processes suppress the rise of functional silos, and help to ensure an improved coordination in between functions.

The Service Lifecycle

ITIL version 3 approaches service management from the lifecycle of a service. The Service Lifecycle is an organization model providing insight into:
- the way service management is structured
- the way the various lifecycle components are linked to each other
- the impact that changes in one component will have on other components and on the entire lifecycle system

So the new ITIL version focuses on the Service Lifecycle, and the way service management components are linked. The processes are also discussed (both the old familiar ones and the new ones) in the cycle phases. They describe how things change.

The Service Lifecycle consists of five phases. Each volume of the new ITIL books describes one of these phases:
- **Service Strategy** - the phase of designing, developing and implementing service management as a strategic resource
- **Service Design** - the design phase of developing appropriate IT services, including architecture, processes, policy and documents; the design goal is to meet the current and future business requirements
- **Service Transition** - the phase of developing and improving capabilities for the transition of new and modified services to production

- **Service Operation** - the phase of achieving effectiveness and efficiency in providing and supporting services in order to ensure value for the customer and the service provider
- **Continual Service Improvement** - the phase of creating and maintaining the value for the customer by design improvement, and service introduction and operation

Service Strategy is the axis of the Service Lifecycle (Figure 2.3) that "runs" all other phases; it is the phase of policymaking and objectives. The phases Service Design, Service Transition and Service Operation implement this strategy, their continual theme is adjustment and change. The Continual Service Improvement phase stands for learning and improving, and embraces all cycle phases. This phase initiates improvement programs and projects, and prioritizes them based on the strategic objectives of the organization.

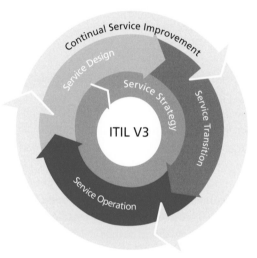

Figure 2.3 The Service Lifecycle

The Service Lifecycle is a combination of many perspectives on the reality of organizations. This offers more flexibility and control.

The dominant pattern in the Service Lifecycle is the succession of Service Strategy to Service Design, to Service Transition and to Service Operation, and then, through Continual Service Improvement, back to Service Strategy, and so on. The cycle encompasses, however, many patterns. Depending on tasks and responsibilities, a manager can choose his own control perspective. If you are responsible for the design, development or improvement of processes, the best perspective to use is a process perspective. If you are responsible for managing SLAs, contracts and services, the Service Lifecycle perspective and its various phases is likely to meet your needs better.

ITIL Library
The official, new style ITIL Library encompasses the following components:
- Core Library - the five Service Lifecycle publications:
  - Service Strategy
  - Service Design
  - Service Transition
  - Service Operation
  - Continual Service Improvement

  Each book covers a phase from the Service Lifecycle and encompasses various processes. The processes are always described in detail in the book in which they find their key application.
- Complementary portfolio:
  - introduction guide
  - key element guides
  - qualification aids
  - white papers
  - glossary

CHAPTER 3

Lifecycle Phase: Service Operation

3.1 Introduction

Well designed and implemented processes are of little value when the day-to-day fulfilment of these processes is not well organized. Nor are service improvements possible when the day-to-day performance measuring and data gathering activities are not fulfilled systematically during the Service Operation.

Objectives

The goals of Service Operation are to coordinate and fulfill activities and processes required to provide and manage services for business users and customers with a specified agreed level. Service Operation is also responsible for management of the technology required to provide and support the services.

Scope

Service Operation is about fulfilling all activities required to provide and support services. These include:

- the services
- the service management processes
- the technology
- the people

Optimizing the Service Operation performance

Service Operation can be improved in two ways:

- Long-term incremental improvement - This is based on the review of the performances and output of all Service Operation processes, functions and outputs over time; examples include putting new tools into use or changes in the design process.

- Short-term ongoing improvement of existing situations within the Service Operation processes, functions and technology - These are small changes that are implemented to change the fundamental significance of a process or technology; examples are tuning, training or staff transfer.

3.2 Basic concepts

Service Operation is responsible for the fulfillment of processes that optimize the service costs and quality in the service management lifecycle. As part of the organization, Service Operation must help ensure that the customer (business) achieves its goals. Additionally, it is responsible for the effective functioning of components supporting the service.

Functions, groups, teams, departments and divisions
The Service Operation book refers, with various terms, to the way people are organized to fulfill processes or activities:

- **function** - a logical concept that refers to the people and automated actions that execute a defined process, an activity or a combination of processes and activities
- **group** - a number of people who are similar to each other in some way; in this book, group refers to people fulfilling similar activities
- **team** - a more formal type of group of people working together to achieve a common goal, for example, project teams or application development teams; this does not necessarily have to take place in the same organizational structure
- **department** - a formal organizational structure that performs a specific series of defined activities
- **division** - refers to a number of departments that are clustered, often based on geographic location or product line
- **role** - refers to a series of connected behaviors or actions that are performed in a specific context by an individual, team or group. A chief system manager can, for example, perform the role of problem manager, and a technical management department can perform the role of technical observation point

Achieving balance in Service Operation

Procedures and activities take place in a continually changing environment. This can give rise to a conflict between maintaining the current situation and reacting to changes in the business and technical environment. Consequently, one of the key roles of Service Operation is handling this conflict. It must try to achieve a balance between conflicting priorities.

The internal IT view versus the external business view

The view that IT is part of IT services (the external business view) is the opposite of the idea that IT is a series of technological components (the internal IT view). This causes the key conflict in all phases of the IT service management lifecycle.

The external IT view is about the way users and customers experience services. The internal IT view is about how the IT organization manages IT components and systems to provide services.

Both views are necessary to provide services. The organization that is exclusively focused on business requirements without thinking about how they will provide services will eventually only make promises they are unable to live up to. An organization that is exclusively focused on internal systems without thinking about which services they will support, will eventually support expensive services that are of little use. It is a matter of achieving a balance between these two extremes (see Figure 3.1).

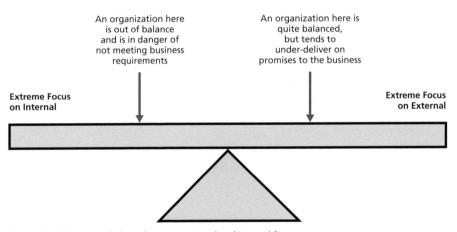

Figure 3.1 Achieving a balance between external and internal focus

Stability versus responsiveness

On the one hand, Service Operation must ensure that the IT infrastructure is stable and available. At the same time, Service Operation must recognize that business and IT requirements change.

Some changes take place gradually and can be planned. They do not jeopardize stability. The platform functionality, performance and architecture will change over a number of years.

However, other changes can happen very quickly, sometimes under extreme pressure. For example, a business department wins a contract that suddenly requires additional IT services and more capacity.

To achieve an IT organization in which stability and response are in balance:
- Invest in adaptable technologies and processes, for example, virtual server and application technology.
- Build a strong service level management process that is active from the Service Design phase to the Continual Service Improvement phase of the IT service management Lifecycle.
- Encourage integration between service level management and the other Service Design processes, so that business requirements match the operational IT activities and components of the IT infrastructure.
- Initiate changes in the IT service management lifecycle as soon as possible; they can be taken into account in the functional and management requirements.
- Involve IT as soon as possible in the change process in case of business changes; this helps ensure scalability, consistency and IT services that include the business changes.
- Have the Service Operation teams provide input for the design and the refining of architecture and IT services.
- Implement and use service level management to prevent that business and IT managers and staff negotiate agreements informally.

Service quality versus service costs
Service Operation must provide IT services to customers and the users continually, and to the agreed level. At the same time, they have to keep the costs and use of resources at an optimal level. Many organizations are strongly pressured to enhance the service quality, while they have to reduce costs.

Achieving an optimal balance between costs and quality is a key task of service management. Many organizations leave this to the Service Operations team, who lack the authority, but the Service Strategy and Service Design phase are more appropriate for this. Service level requirements and a clear understanding of the goals and dangers of service business can help ensure that the service is provided with the right costs.

Reactive versus proactive

A reactive organization does nothing until an external stimulus forces it to act. For instance, it only develops a new application when a new business requirement demands. A proactive organization always looks for new opportunities to improve the current situation. Usually, proactive behavior is viewed positively, because it enables the organization to keep a competitive advantage in a changing environment. An over-proactive attitude can be very costly, and can create distracted staff. For an optimal result, reactive and proactive behavior must be well-balanced.

Providing a service

All Service Operation staff members must be aware that they are providing a service to the business. Do not only train staff to provide and support IT services, but also teach them the attitude with which they should provide these services.

Involving operational staff in design and transition

It is very important that the Service Operation staff are involved in Service Design and Service Transition, and, if necessary, in Service Strategy.

One way to achieve a balance in Service Operation is an effective set of Service Design processes. This will provide IT operations management with:
- a clear definition of IT service goals and performance criteria
- a link between IT service specifications and the IT infrastructure performance
- a definition of the operational performance requirements
- service and technology planning
- the ability to model the impact of changes in technology and business requirements
- an appropriate cost model to review the return on investment (ROI), and cost reduction strategies

Operational health

An organization can determine its operational health by isolating some "vital characteristics" of devices or services that are essential to the execution of a critical business function. Consider, for example, the bandwidth usage on a network segment, or the memory usage on an important server. If the value of these characteristics lies within the normal system range, the system is sound, and will not require any additional attention.

From time to time though, it is necessary to check the systems thoroughly for problems that do not directly affect the vital characteristics. The operational soundness also depends on the ability to prevent incidents and problems. Invest in a reliable and well-maintainable infrastructure for this. Create a solid availability design and practice proactive problem management.

Finally, the operational health depends on the ability to identify and effectively locate defects once they have occurred, so that they have little impact on the service. This also requires a solid incident and problem management.

Communication
IT teams and departments, as well as users, internal customer and Service Operation teams, have to communicate effectively with each other. Good communication can prevent problems. Any communication must have a certain goal or result. Every team and every department must have a clear communications policy.

Service Operation has various types of communication:
* routine operational communication
* communication between shifts
* performance reports
* communication during projects
* communication in case of changes
* communication in case of exceptions
* communication in case of emergencies
* training on new or adjusted processes and service designs
* communication of Service Strategy and Service Design with Service Operation teams

Documentation
IT operation management and all technical and application management teams and departments are involved in recording and maintaining the following documents:
* process manuals for all the processes they are involved with
* technical procedure manuals
* planning documents such as capacity and availability plans
* service portfolio
* work instructions for the service management tools, in order to comply with the reporting requirements

3.3   Processes and other activities

This section devotes its attention to the following processes, activities and functions:
- event management
- incident management
- problem management
- request fulfilment
- access management
- monitoring and control (activity)
- IT operations (function)

Additionally, there are other processes that will be executed or supported during Service Operation, but are driven by other phases of the service management lifecycle:
- change management
- capacity management
- availability management
- financial management
- knowledge management
- IT Service Continuity Management (ITSCM)
- service reporting and measurement

Event management

An event is an occurrence that affects the IT infrastructure management or the provision of an IT service. For the most part, events are notifications created by an IT service, configuration item or monitoring tool. For an effective Service Operation, the organization must know its infrastructure status, and be able to trace deviations of the regular or expected performance. Good monitoring and control systems provide information for this.

Event management surveys all events that occur in the IT infrastructure in order to monitor the regular performance, and which can be automated to trace and escalate unforeseen circumstances.

Event management can be applied to any aspect of service management that must be managed and can be automated.

The most important activities of the event management process are:
- event occurs
- event notification
- event detection

- event filtering
- the event significance (event classification)
- event correlation
- trigger
- response selection
- action assessment
- close event

There is no standard record for event management; metrics should be set accordingly.

Incident management

The incident management process focuses on restoring failure of service as quickly as possible for customers, so that it has a minimal impact on the business. Incidents can be failures, questions or queries.

Incident management includes any event that interrupts or can interrupt a service; so they also include events reported by customers, either by the service desk or through various tools.

The incident management process consists of the following steps:
- identifying
- recording/logging
- categorizing
- prioritizing
- initial diagnosing
- escalating
- investigating and diagnosing
- resolving and restoring
- closing

Request fulfilment

Request fulfilment is the process of handling service requests, where a separate process is utilized that initiates the need for a request. Most of the time, it concerns small changes that initially pass through the service desk.

The goals of the request fulfilment process are:
- offering users a channel where they can request and receive standard services; there must be an agreed approval and qualification process for this

- providing information to customers about the availability of services and the procedure to obtain them
- providing the standard services components (such as licenses and software media)
- assisting with general information, complaints or remarks

Request fulfilment consists of the following activities, methods and techniques:
- menu selection
- financial approval
- other approval
- fulfilment
- closure

Problem management
Problem management is responsible for analyzing and resolving the causes of incidents. In addition, it develops proactive activities to prevent current and future incidents, using a so-called "known error sub process" that enables a quicker diagnosis when new incidents happen.

Problem management includes all activities that are needed for a diagnosis of the underlying cause of incidents, and to determine a resolution for those problems. It must also ensure that the resolution is implemented through the appropriate control procedures (i.e. with change management and release management).

Problem management consists of two important processes:
- reactive problem management
- proactive problem management

Reactive problem management consists of:
- detection
- logging
- categorizing
- prioritizing
- investigating and diagnosing
- determining workarounds
- identifying a known error
- finding a resolution
- closing
- reviewing major problems
- mistakes in development environment

Access management

Access management is the process of allowing authorized users access to use a service, while access of unauthorized users is limited. In some organizations this is also known as rights or identity management.

Access management helps ensure that this access is always available at agreed times. This is provided by availability management.

A service request through the help desk can initiate access management.

Access management consists of:
- requesting access
- verification
- assigning rights
- monitoring of the identity status
- logging and tracking access
- removing or restricting rights

Monitoring and control

Service monitoring and control is based on a continual cycle of monitoring, reporting and undertaking action. This cycle is crucial to providing, supporting and improving services.

Monitoring and control cycle

The best-known model for describing control is the **monitor control loop**. Although a simple model, it has many complex applications in IT service management.

There are two types of monitoring and control cycles:
- open loop systems
- closed loop systems

There are two monitoring levels:
- internal monitoring and control
- external monitoring and control

In practice, many organizations have combinations of internal and external monitoring, but in many cases they are not linked.

There are various types of monitoring tools; the situation determines which **type of monitoring** is adopted.

IT operations
IT Operations activities refer to the day-to-day operational activities that are needed to manage the IT infrastructure.

Console management/operations bridge
The operations bridge is a central coordination point that controls various events and routine operational activities; it detects incidents and reports the performance status of technological components.

An operations bridge gathers all the crucial observation points in the IT infrastructure, so that they can be monitored and controlled from a central location with minimum effort.

The operations bridge combines many activities such as console management, event handling, first-line network management, job scheduling and support after regular office hours. In some organizations, the service desk is part of the operations bridge.

Job scheduling
IT Operations perform the standard routines, queries or reports that technical management and application management teams have transferred as part of the service or as part of routine day-to-day maintenance tasks.

Backup and restore
Backup and restore is essentially a component of well planned continuity. Service Design must help to ensure that there are good backup strategies for each service. Service Transition must help to ensure that they are tested correctly. The only point of taking backups is to ensure that information can be restored.

Other operational activities
The remainder of this section focuses on a number of operational activities which ensure that the technology matches the service and process goals. Sometimes these activities are described as processes, but they actually concern a series of specialized technical activities that help to ensure that the technology needed for providing support to the services works effectively and efficiently.

Mainframe management

Mainframes form the central part of many services, and their performance forms a baseline for service performance and user and customer expectations.

The way in which mainframe management teams are organized varies substantially. In some organizations a specialized team fulfills all aspects of mainframe management. In other organizations this is done by several teams or departments.

Server management and support

Most organizations use servers to offer flexible and accessible services for hosting applications or databases, fulfilling client/server services, storage, print and file management.

The server team or department must fulfil the following procedures and activities:
- supporting the operating system
- license management for all configuration items
- third-line support
- procurement advice
- system security
- definition and management of virtual servers
- capacity and performance

Network management

Since most IT services are dependent on connectivity, network management is crucial to service provision. Service Operation staff access important service components, via network management.

Network management is responsible for all Local Area Networks (LANs), Metropolitan Area Networks (MANs) and Wide Area Networks (WANs) within an organization.

Storage and archiving

Many services require that data must be stored for a specific time. Often, such data must be made available as an offline archive when it is no longer required on a daily basis. This is not only for compliance with external regulations and legislation, but also because data may be invaluable internally to an organization for a variety of other reasons.

Storage and archiving does not only demand infrastructure component management, but also policy that prescribes where data must be stored, for how long, in which form, and who can access the data.

Database administration
Database administration must work closely together with key application management teams or departments. In some organizations the functions can be combined or can be brought under one management structure.

Database administration must ensure optimal database performance, security and functionality. Database administrators have, among others, the following responsibilities:
• designing and maintaining database standards and policies
• database design, creation and testing

Directory services management
A directory service is a specialized software application that manages information about the available resources on a network, and to which users it is accessible. It is the basis for providing access to those resources, and for detecting and preventing unauthorized access.

Directory services look at every resource as an object of the directory server, and name them. Every name will be linked to a resource network address, so that users do not have to remember confusing and complex addresses.

Desktop support
Many users have access to IT services through a desktop or laptop. Desktop support is responsible for all desktop and laptop hardware, software and peripheral equipment in an organization. Specific responsibilities include:
• **desktop policy and procedures** - for example, license policy, personal use of laptops and desktops, etc.
• **desktop maintenance** - such as release implementation, upgrades, patches and hot fixes
• **support of connectivity problems** (together with network management) - for home-workers and field staff

Middleware management
Middleware connects software components, or integrates them with distributed or unlike applications and systems. Middleware enables effective data transfer between applications. For this reason middleware is important for services that depend on multiple applications or data resources. This is especially relevant in the context of service orientated software/architecture (SOA).

Internet/web management
Many organizations use the internet for their business operations, and are therefore heavily dependent upon the availability and performance of their websites. In such cases, a separate internet/web support team is required. This team has, among others, the following tasks:
- designing internet and web services architecture
- the specification of standards for the development and management of web based applications, content, websites and web pages; this is usually addressed during Service Design
- maintaining all web development and management applications
- supporting interfaces with back-end and legacy systems
- monitoring and managing web based performance, such as user experience simulation, benchmarking and virtualization

Facility and data center management
Facility management refers to management of the physical environment of IT operations, which are usually located in data centers or computer rooms. This is an extensive and complex subject. Service Operation only provides an overview of the most important roles and activities, and emphasizes the role of facility management in data center management.

Data center strategies
Managing a data center is much more than hosting an open room where technical groups install and manage equipment for which they use their own approach and procedures. It requires a series of processes and procedures; it involves all IT groups in every phase of the IT service management lifecycle. Data center activities are determined by strategic and design decisions about management and control, and are fulfilled by operators.

Information security management and Service Operation
Service Design discusses information security management as process. Information security management is responsible for setting policy, standards and procedures that ensure protection of organization assets, data, information and IT services. Service Operation teams play a role in fulfilling these policy regulations, standards and procedures, and work closely together with the teams or departments that are responsible for information security management. The role of a service operation team consists of:
- **Policing and reporting** - Operational staff check system journals, logs, event/ monitoring alerts, hacker detections and actual or potential security breach reports; to do this, they work closely with information security management; this is how a

"check and balance system" comes into existence, which ensures effective detection and control of security issues.

- **Technical assistance** - Sometimes IT security staff need support for their security incident research, for report creation or for gathering forensic evidence that will be used for disciplinary actions or criminal prosecution.
- **Operational security management** - For operational reasons technical staff need access to important technical areas (root system passwords, physical entry into data centers or communication rooms, etc.); it is crucial that all these activities are checked and recorded so that security events can be detected and prevented.
- **Screening and vetting** - To ensure that every member of the Service Operation staff will meet the security requirements of the organization, each member's background is checked; the background of service providers and third parties may also need to be security cleared.
- **Training and awareness** - Service Operation staff must be trained regularly in the security policy and the procedures of an organization; this cultivates awareness; this training must include details on disciplinary actions.

Operational activity improvement
Service Operation staff must be looking continually for process improvement opportunities in order to achieve a higher service quality or a more efficient service provision. This can be done with the following activities:
- automating manual tasks
- reviewing makeshift activities or activities
- operational audits
- utilizing incident and problem management
- communicating
- education and training

3.4   Organization

Functions
A function is a logical concept that refers to the people and automated measures that execute a defined process, an activity or a combination of processes and activities.

Figure 3.2 shows the service operation functions needed to manage a stable operational IT environment.

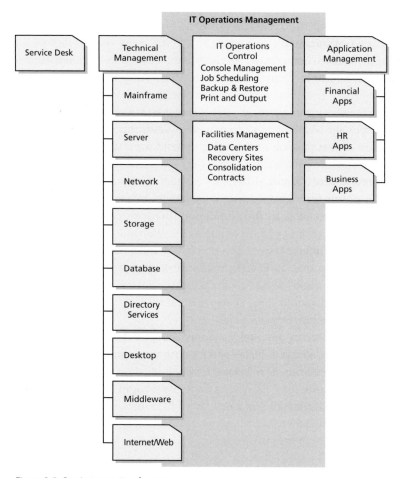

Figure 3.2 Service operation functions

Functions and activities

Due to the technical character and special nature of certain functions, teams, groups and departments are often named after the activities that they undertake. Thus network management is often fulfilled by a network management department. However, this is not an absolute rule. There are a few options available when assigning activities to a team or department:

- an activity can be performed by several teams or departments
- a department can perform several activities
- an activity can be performed by groups

Service desk

A service desk is a **functional unit** with a number of staff members who deal with a variety of service events. Requests may come in through phone calls, the internet or as automatically reported infrastructure events.

The service desk is a very important part of the organization's IT department. It should be the prime contact point for IT users, and it processes all incidents and service requests. Often the staff use software tools to record and manage events.

Justification and the role of a service desk

Many organizations consider a service desk as the best resource for first-line support of IT problems. A service desk provides the following advantages:

- improved customer service, improved customer perception of the service and increased customer satisfaction
- increased accessibility due to a single point of contact, communication and information
- customer and user requests are resolved better and faster
- improved cooperation and communication
- an improved focus on service and a proactive service approach
- reduced negative business impact
- improved infrastructure management and control
- improved use of resources for IT support, and increased business staff productivity
- more meaningful management information for decision support
- it is a good entry position for IT staff

Service desk objectives

The principal goal of the service desk is to restore the "normal service" for users as soon as possible. This could entail resolving a technical error, fulfilling a service request or answering a question.

Organizational structure of a service desk

There are all sorts of ways to structure a service desk. The solution will vary for each organization. The most important options are:

- local service desk
- centralized service desk
- virtual service desk
- follow the sun - "24/7" service
- specialized service desk groups

A local service desk example

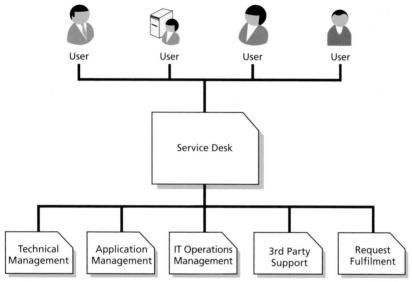

Figure 3.3 A local service desk

A virtual service desk example

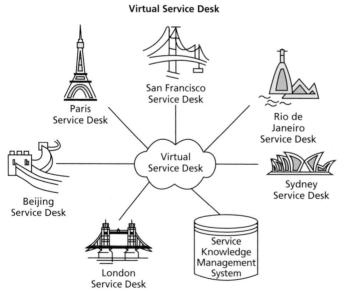

Figure 3.4 A virtual service desk

Service desk staff

It is important to ensure the availability of the correct **number of staff members**, so that the service desk can meet the business demands at any time. The number of calls can fluctuate significantly each day and from hour to hour. When scheduling, a successful organization takes both the peak hours and the slow times into account.

The necessary levels and skills required for service desk staff are also important. The agreed solution times should be balanced against the complexity of the supported systems and "what the business is willing to pay" to determine the required **skill level**. Most of the time, the optimal and most cost-effective approach is first-line support through the service desk, which records the calls and transfers escalations quickly to the second-line and third-line support groups who have more expertise. However, this basic starting point can be improved over time by providing first-line staff with an effective knowledge-base, diagnostics scripts and integrated tools as well as ongoing training and awareness, so that first-line resolution rates can be increased.

Metrics for the service desk

Define realistic **metrics** to review the service desk performance at regular points in time. This way, the maturity, efficiency, effectiveness and opportunities can be assessed, and the service desk activities improved. Do ensure that the service desk performance metrics are realistic and carefully selected.

In addition to the "hard" measurements of the service desk performance, it is also important to conduct "soft" measurements in the form of customer and user satisfaction surveys. Do customers and users think that their calls are answered correctly, was the service desk agent friendly and professional? This type of measurement can best be answered by the user.

Service desk outsourcing

The decision to outsource is a strategic topic for senior managers, and will be discussed in detail in the domains of Service Strategy and Service Design.

Technical management

Technical management refers to the **groups, departments or teams** who offer technical expertise and general management of the IT infrastructure.

The role of technical management

Technical management has a dual role:

- It is the custodian of technical knowledge and expertise in relation to managing the IT infrastructure. In this role, technical management helps ensure that the knowledge required for designing, testing, managing and improving IT services is established, developed and refined.
- It takes care of the actual resources that are needed to support the IT service management lifecycle. In this role, technical management helps ensure that the resources are trained and implemented effectively, so that it can design, build, transfer, process and improve the required technology that is needed to provide and support IT services.

By fulfilling these two roles, technical management helps ensure that the organization is able to access the correct type and level of human resources to manage the technology, and consequently, meet the business goals.

Technical management also drives IT operations while managing the technology operations and providing guidance to IT operations.

Objectives of technical management
Technical management assists in the planning, implementation and maintenance of a stable technical infrastructure to support the organization's business processes. This is done by:
- well-designed and cost-effective technical topology
- using the appropriate technical skills to maintain the technical infrastructure in a optimal condition
- using technical skills effectively, to diagnose and resolve technical failures quickly

General technical management activities
Technical management is involved in several general activities, such as:
- starting training programs
- designing and carrying out training for users, the service desk and other groups
- researching and developing resolutions that may help to expand the service portfolio, or may be used to simplify or automate IT operations
- releases that are often implemented with the assistance of technical management staff

The technical management organization
Generally speaking, technical management is not provided by one department or group. One or more technical support teams are needed to provide technical management and support for the IT infrastructure.

IT operations management consists of a number of technological areas. Each area requires a specific set of skills to manage and operate it. Some skills are related to each other, and can be performed by generalists, while others apply specifically to a component, system or platform.

Technical design and technical maintenance and support

Technical management consists of specialized technical architects, designers, maintenance specialists and support staff.

Metrics for technical management

Specific metrics for technical management depend largely on which technology is being managed. Some general metrics include:
- measuring the agreed output
- process values
- technological performance
- Mean Time Between Failures (MTBF) of specific equipment
- maintenance activity measurement
- training and skill development

Technical management documentation

Among others, technical management documentation consists of:
- technical documentation (manuals, management and administration manuals, user manuals for CIs)
- maintenance schedules
- an inventory of skills

IT operations management

IT operations management is the **function** that is responsible for performing the day-to-day operational activities. They ensure that the agreed level of IT service is provided to the business.

IT operations management plays a dual role:
- It is responsible for implementation of activities and performance standards that have been defined during Service Design and have been tested during Service Transition. In this sense, the role of IT operations focuses on maintaining the status quo, whereby stability of the IT infrastructure and consistency of IT services are the most important tasks of IT operations.

- Simultaneously, IT operations is part of the process that adds value to the business and supports the value network (see *Service Strategy*). IT operations must be capable of continual adaptation to business requirements and demands.

IT operations management objectives
Objectives of IT operations management are:
- maintaining the existing situation to achieve stability in the processes and activities of the organization
- continual research and improvement to achieve better service at lower costs while maintaining stability
- rapid application of operational skills to analyze operational failures and to resolve them

IT operations management organization
IT operations management is seen as a separate function, but in many cases technical and application management workers contribute to this function.
The assignment of activities depends on the maturity of the organization.

IT operations management metrics
IT operations management measures both the effective implementation of defined activities and procedures, as well as execution of process activities. Examples include:
- successful completion of planned tasks
- the number of exceptions to planned activities and tasks
- process metrics
- metrics of maintenance activities
- metrics related to facility management

IT operations management documentation
IT operations management generates and uses a number of documents, including:
- **Standard Operating Procedures (SOP)** - A series of documents providing detailed instructions and activity schedules for each IT operations management team, department or group.
- **Operations logs** - Each activity that is performed as part of IT operations must be registered for a variety of reasons, in order to:
  - confirm successful completion of specific tasks or activities
  - confirm that an IT service was provided as agreed
  - provide a basis for problem management to research the underlying cause of incidents
  - provide a basis for reports about performance of IT operations teams and departments

- **Shift schedules and reports** - Documents that display the exact activities that must be performed during a shift; there is also a list showing all dependencies and the sequence of activities; there may be more than one operational schedule because each team may be provided with a version for its own systems.

Application management

Application management is responsible for the management of applications during their lifecycle. The application management **function** is executed by a department, group or team that is involved with management and support of operational applications. Application management also plays an important role in designing, testing and improving applications that are part of IT services.

Application management role

Application management is for applications what technical management is for IT infrastructure. It plays a role in all applications, whether they are purchased or have been internally developed. One of the most important decisions to which they contribute is whether to purchase an application or to develop it internally (discussed in detail in Service Design). When this decision has been made, application management plays a dual role:

- it is the custodian of technical knowledge and expertise for the management of applications
- it provides actual resources for the support of the IT service management lifecycle

Two other roles filled by application management:

- it provides advice to IT operations about the best way to carry out the ongoing operational management of applications
- it integrates the Application Management Lifecycle with the IT service management lifecycle

Application management objectives

The objectives of application management are to support the business processes of the organization by determining functional and management requirements for applications. Another objective is to assist in design and implementation of the applications and to support and improve them.

Application management principles

One of the most important decisions in application management is whether to **develop or purchase** an application which supports the requested functionality. The Chief Technical Officer (CTO), or steering group, makes the ultimate decision, but in doing so, both depend on a number of information sources. If the decision maker wants to have the application developed, they will also have to decide whether to have it developed by staff or to outsource the development. This is further discussed in detail in Service Design.

Application management lifecycle
The lifecycle that is followed to develop and manage the application goes by many names, such as the Software Lifecycle (SLC) and the Software Development Lifecycle (SDLC). These are mostly used by application development teams and their project managers to define their involvement in designing, developing, testing, implementing and supporting applications. Examples of this approach include Structured Systems Analysis and Design Methodology (SSADM) and Dynamic Systems Development Method (DSDM).

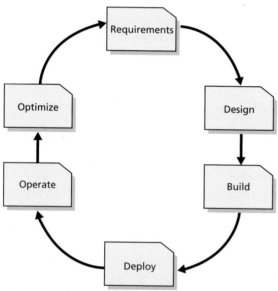

Figure 3.5 Application management lifecycle

Application development and operations are part of the same lifecycle and must be involved through all Service Lifecycle phases, although the degree of involvement depends on the lifecycle phase.

> **Relation between application management lifecycle and service management lifecycle**
>
> The application management lifecycle is not an alternative for the service management lifecycle. Applications are part of services and must be managed as such. Nevertheless, applications are a unique mix of technology and functionality and this requires a special focus during each phase of the service management lifecycle.
>
> Each phase of the application management lifecycle has its own specific objectives, activities, deliverables and dedicated teams. Each phase also has a clear responsibility to ensure that its output corresponds with the specific objectives of the service management lifecycle.

The phases of applications management within Service Operation are:
- requirements
- design
- build
- deploy
- operate
- optimize

During the first phase, the **requirements** for a new application are collected, based on the business needs of the organization. There are six requirement types for an application, whether it is developed in-house, outsourced or purchased:
- **functional requirements** - what is necessary to support a certain business function?
- **management requirements** - concentrate on the need for responsive, available and secure service, and involve things like deployment, system management, and security
- **usability requirements** - what are the needs of the user, and how can they be satisfied?
- **architecture requirements** - especially if it requires a change in the existing architecture standards
- **interface requirements** - where dependencies occur between existing applications or tools and the new application
- **service level requirements** - specify how the service is to be delivered, what the quality of the output has to be and other qualitative aspects that are measured by the user or client

The **design phase** will translate the requirements into specifications. Design of the application and the environment or the operational model in which the application is run will also take place during the Design Phase. Architectural considerations for design and operation are the most important aspect of this phase, because they can impact the structure and content of both the application and the operational model.

The **build phase** gets the application and the operational model ready for deployment. Application components are coded and purchased, integrated and tested. Testing is not a separate phase in the lifecycle although it is a separate activity. Testing forms an integral part of the development and roll-out phase, as validation of the activity and output of those phases. This is known as the Early Life Support (more information on this topic can be found in Service Transition).

The **deployment phase** deploys the operational model and the application. The existing IT environment absorbs the operational model and the application is installed on top of the operational model. This involves the processes of release and deployment management that are described under Service Transition.

During the **operate phase** the service organization uses the application as part of providing services requested by the business. The performance of the application in relation to the total service is measured continually in relation to the service levels and the most important business drivers.

The **optimize phase** reviews and analyzes the results of the service level performance metrics. Possible improvements are discussed and the necessary developments are initiated. The two main strategies involve maintaining and iteratively improving service levels at lower costs. This can lead to a change in the lifecycle of an application or to its retirement. Good communication with users is important during this phase.

Generic application management activities
Although most application management teams and departments are dedicated to specific applications, they share a number of activities. These include:
- identifying the knowledge needed to manage and operate applications in the Service Operation phase
- initiating training programs to develop and refine skills in the appropriate application management resources and to maintain training reports for these resources
- defining standards for designing new architectures and determining application architectures during Service Strategy processes

- testing, designing and executing the functionality, performance and controllability of IT services
- defining event management standards
- defining, managing and maintaining attributes and relations of application CIs in the configuration management system

Application management organization
Although application management departments, groups and teams all perform similar functions, each application has its own set of management and operational requirements. Differences may include:
- the purpose of the application
- the functionality of the application
- the platform on which the application is run
- the type or the brand of technology that is used

Application management teams and departments are mostly organized on the basis of the categories of the applications that they support. Examples of typical application management organization include:
- financial applications
- HR applications
- manufacturing support
- sales support
- call center and marketing applications
- business specific applications
- IT applications
- web portals

Traditionally, application development and management teams / departments have operated as autonomous units. Each team manages its own environment in its own way and they all have a separate interface to the business. Recent attention for object-oriented and *Service Oriented Architectures* and the growing pressure from business that demands a faster response and improved cooperation has brought these two worlds closer together. This requires a higher involvement of Service Operational personnel in the Service Design phase.

Application management roles and responsibilities
Application management has two roles:
- **the application manager** - supervises and has overall responsibility for management and the decisions that are made

* **the application analyst/architect** - is responsible for requirements that meet the application specifications

Application management metrics
The application management metrics mainly depend on the way in which the applications are managed, but general metrics include:
* measuring agreed-upon outputs
* process metrics
* performance of the application
* measuring maintenance activities
* application management teams cooperate closely with application development teams and the correct metrics must be used to measure this
* training and skill development

Service Operation roles and responsibilities
The key to effective ITSM is ensuring that there is clear accountability and roles defined to carry out the practice of Service Operation.

Service desk roles
The following roles are needed for the service desk:
* **service desk manager**
    - manages service desk activities
    - acts as escalation point for supervisors
    - takes on wider customer service role
    - reports to senior managers about any issue that could significantly impact the business
    - attends Change Advisory Board meetings
    - overall responsibility for processing incidents and service requests
* **service desk supervisor**
    - ensures that staffing and skill levels are maintained
    - is responsible for production of management reports
    - acts as escalation point for difficult calls
* **service desk analysts**
    - deliver first line support by accepting calls and processing the resulting incidents or service requests, using incident and request fulfilment processes
* **super users**
    - business users who act as liaison points between business and IT

Technical management roles

The following roles are needed for the technical management areas:
- technical managers / team leaders
  - responsible for leadership, control and decision-making
- technical analysts / architects
  - defining and maintaining knowledge on how systems are related and ensuring that dependencies are understood
- technical operators
  - performing day-to-day operational tasks

IT Operation management roles

The following roles are needed for IT Operations management:
- IT operations manager
- shift leader
- IT operations analysts
- IT operators

Application management roles

Application management requires Application Managers and Team Leaders. They have overall responsibility for leadership, control and decision making for the applications team or department.

Application Analysts and Architects are responsible for matching business requirements to technical specifications.

Event management roles

It is unusual to appoint an "event manager" but it is important that event management procedures are coordinated. The service desk is not typically involved in event management, but if events have been identified as incidents, the service desk will escalate them to the appropriate service operation teams.

Technical and application management play an important role in event management. For example, the teams will perform event management for the systems under their control.

Incident management roles

The **incident manager** is responsible for:

- driving the effectiveness and efficiency of the incident management process
- producing management information
- managing the work of incident support staff (first tier and second tier)
- monitoring the effectiveness of incident management and making recommendations for improvement
- managing major incidents
- developing and maintaining incident management systems and processes
- effectively managing incidents using first, second, and third tier support

Request fulfilment roles

Initial service request handling is done by the service desk and incident management staff. Actual fulfilment will be undertaken by the appropriate service operation team(s) or departments and/or external suppliers.

Problem management roles

One person (or, in larger organizations, a team) should be responsible for problem management. The **problem manager** is responsible for coordinating all problem management activities and is specifically responsible for:

- liaison with all problem resolution groups to accomplish quick solutions to problems within SLA targets
- ownership and protection of the Known Error Database
- formal closure of all problem records
- liaison with vendors and other parties to ensure compliance with contractual obligations
- managing, executing, documenting and planning all (follow-up) activities that relate to major problem reviews

Access management roles

Since access management is the execution of security and availability management, these two areas will be responsible for defining the appropriate roles. Although usually no access manager is appointed by an organization, it is important there should be one process for managing privileges and access. This process and the related policy are usually defined and maintained by information security management and executed by various service operation functions, such as the service desk, technical management and application management.

Service Operation organization structures

There are several ways to organize Service Operation functions, and each organization will come to its own decisions based on its size, geography, culture and business environment.

Organization by technical specialization

This organization type creates departments according to the technology, the skills and activities necessary to manage that technology. IT operations follows the structure of the technical management and application management departments. As a consequence IT operations is geared to the operational agendas of the technical management and application management departments, and all groups have to be defined during the Service Design phase.

Organization by activity

This type of organization structure focuses on the fact that similar activities are performed on all technologies within an organization. This means that people who perform similar activities, regardless of the technology, are grouped together, although teams may occur within each department that is involved with a specific technology, application, etc.

Organizing to manage processes

It is not a good idea to structure the entire organization according to processes. Processes are used to eliminate the "silo effect" of departments, not to create silos.

In process-based organizations, people are organized in groups or departments that perform or manage a specific process. However, this type of organization structure should only be used if IT operations management is responsible for more than IT operations. In some organizations IT operations is also responsible for defining SLAs and negotiating UCs.

Process-based departments are only effective if they are capable of coordinating process execution throughout the entire organization. This means that process-based departments can only be considered if IT operations management can play the role of process owner for specific processes.

Organizing IT operation by geography

IT operations can be physically spread out, and in some cases each location must be organized according to its own context. This structure is usually used in the following circumstances, when:
- data centers are geographically distributed

- different regions or countries possess different technologies or offer a different range of services
- there are different business models or organizational structures in the different regions; in other words, the business is decentralized according to geography and the each business unit is fairly autonomous
- legislation differs between country or region
- different standards apply, per country or region
- there are cultural or language differences between the personnel who are managing IT

Hybrid organization structures
It is unlikely that IT operations management will be structured using only one type of organizational structure. Most organizations use a technical specialization combined with some extra activity or process-based departments:
- **Combined functions** - The IT operations, technical management and application management departments are included in one structure; this sometimes occurs when all groups are co-located in one data center; in these situations, the data center manager assumes responsibility for technical, application and IT production management.
- **Combined technical and application management structure** - Some businesses organize their technical management and application management functions according to systems; this means that every department contains application specialists and IT infrastructure technical specialists who manage services based on a series of systems.

3.5 Methods, techniques and tools
The most important requirements for Service Operation are:
- an integrated IT service management technology (or toolset)
- self-help (e.g. FAQ's on a web interface)
- workflow or process management engine
- an integrated CMS
- discovery/deployment/licensing technology
- remote control
- diagnostic utilities
- reporting capabilities
- dashboards
- integration with business service management

3.6 Implementation

General implementation guidelines for Service Operation:

Managing change in Service Operation

Service Operation staff must implement changes without negative impact on the stability of offered IT services.

Change triggers

There are many things that can trigger change in the Service Operation environment, including:

- new or to be upgraded hardware or software
- legislation
- obsolete components
- business imperatives
- process enhancements
- changes in management or personnel
- change in service levels
- new services

Change assessment

Involve Service Operation as early as possible in assessment of all changes. This way, operational issues will be handled properly.

Assessing and managing risk in Service Operation

In a number of cases, it is necessary that risk evaluation is conducted swiftly, in order to take appropriate action. This is especially necessary for potential changes or known errors, but also in case of failures, projects, environmental risks, vendors, security risks and new clients that need support.

Operational staff in Service Design and Transition

Service Operation staff should be particularly involved in the early stages of Service Design and Transition. This will ensure that the new services will actually work in practice and that they can be supported by Service Operation staff.

Planning and implementation of service management technologies

There are several factors that organizations must plan before and during deployment of ITSM support tools, such as:

- licenses
- deployment

- capacity checks
- timing of technology deployment
- the type of introduction - the choice of a big-bang introduction or a phased approach

Next, we will discuss some challenges that Service Operation must overcome.

Lack of engagement with development and project staff
Historically, there is a separation between Service Operation staff and staff involved in the development of new applications or in the execution of projects that deliver new functionality in an operational environment.

This image is damaging because contemplating Service Operation issues is best done at the beginning of new developments or projects, when there is still time to include these factors in the planning stages.

Service Design and Service Transition describe the steps necessary to include IT production issues in new developments and projects right from the start.

Justifying funding
Often is it difficult to justify expenditure for Service Operation because funds spent are often considered to be "infrastructure" costs.

In reality, many investments in IT service management, especially for Service Operation, can save money and show a positive ROI as well as improving service quality.

Challenges for Service Operation managers
Managers in Service Operation can be faced with the following challenges:
- Service Design has the tendency to focus on one service while Service Operation aims at delivering and supporting all services.
- Service Design will often be conducted in projects while Service Operation focuses on continual management processes and activities that recur.
- The two phases of the lifecycle possess different metrics that encourage Service Design to conclude the project on time, as specified and within the arranged budget. However, it is hard to predict how the service will look, and what will be the costs after roll-out and some initial time in service. If the service does not work as expected, IT operations management will be responsible.
- Ineffective Service Transition may hamper the transition from design to production.

Another series of challenges involves metrics. Each alternative structure will introduce a different combination of items that can be easy or difficult to measure.

A third set of challenges concerns the use of virtual teams. Traditional, hierarchical management structures are unable to handle the complexity and diversity of most organizations. Knowledge management and mapping authority structures becomes increasingly important as organizations expand and diversify. Service Strategy will expand on this further.

One of the most important challenges facing Service Operation managers is the balance between the many internal and external relationships. There is an increasing use of networks, partnerships and shared services models. A Service Operation manager must invest in relation management knowledge and skills in order to handle the complexity of these challenges.

Critical success factors

Management support
Support from higher and middle management is necessary for all IT service management activities and processes, especially in Service Operation. It is crucial for obtaining sufficient financing and resources. Senior management must also offer visible support during the launch of new Service Operation initiatives.

Middle management must also provide the necessary support and actions.

Business support
It is also important that Service Operation is supported by the business units. This works better if the Service Operation staff involve the business in all their activities, and are open about successes and failures.

Regular communication with the business is crucial to building a good relationship and to ensuring support; Service Operation will be better placed to understand the aspirations and concerns of the business. Additionally, the business can provide feedback on the efforts of Service Operation to satisfy the business needs.

Hiring and retaining staff
The correct number of staff with the correct skills is critical for successful Service Operation. Consider the following challenges:

- Projects for new services often clearly specify what the new skills must be, but may underestimate how many staff are needed and how skills can be retained.
- There may be a lack of staff with solid knowledge of service management; having good technicians is important, but there must also be a certain number of people who have knowledge of both technological and service problems.
- Because staff with both technological and service knowledge are fairly rare, they are often specially trained; it is important to retain them by offering a clear career path and solid compensation.
- Staff are often assigned new tasks too quickly, while they are still extremely busy with their current workloads. Successful service management projects may require a short term investment in temporary workers.

Service management training

Good training and awareness can provide great advantages. In addition to increasing expertise, they can generate enthusiasm in people. Service Operation staff must be aware of the consequences of their actions for the organization. A "service management culture" must be created. Service management will only be successful if the people are focused on overall service management objectives.

Appropriate tools

Many service management processes and activities cannot be effectively executed without proper support tools. Senior management must ensure that financing for such tools is included in annual budgets, and must support acquisition, implementation and maintenance.

Test validity

The quality of IT services provided by Service Operation depends on the quality of systems and components that are delivered in the operational environment.

The quality level will improve considerably if solid and complete testing of new components and releases is performed in a timely manner. Also, the documentation should be independently tested for completeness and quality.

Measuring and reporting

Clear agreements are necessary regarding the way in which things are measured and reported; all staff will have clear targets to aim for, and IT and business managers will be able to evaluate quickly and simply whether progress is being made and which areas deserve extra attention.

Risks

Consider the following risks:

- **Service loss** - The greatest risk run by Service Operation is the loss of essential IT services with adverse impact on staff, customers and finances. In extreme cases, loss may occur to life and health, when IT services are used for essential health and security purposes.
- **Risks to successful Service Operation**:
  - insufficient financing and resources
  - loss of momentum
  - loss of important staff
  - resistance to change
  - lack of management support
  - if the design fails the requirements, successful implementation will never deliver the required results; this will require new design
  - in some organizations, service management is viewed with suspicion by both IT and the business; the advantages of service management must be clear for all stakeholders; this problem can be solved by clear service level management and careful communication during Service Design

CHAPTER 4

Introduction to Functions and Processes

4.1 Introduction

Processes are *internal* affairs for the IT service provider. An organization that is still trying to gain control of its processes therefore has an **internal focus**. Organizations that focus on gaining control of their systems in order to provide services are still internally focused. The organization is not ready for an **external focus** until it controls its services and is able to vary them on request. This external focus is required to evolve into that desirable customer-focused organization.

Because organizations can be in different stages of maturity, IT managers require a broad orientation in their discipline. Most organizations are now working on the introduction of a process-focused or customer-focused approach, or still have to start working on this. Process control is therefore a vital step on the road towards a **mature customer-focused organization**.

ITIL has made an important contribution to the organization of that process-focused operating method in the past decade. The development started in North-western Europe and has made some progress on most other continents in the last few years also. On a global scale, however, a minimal number of organizations have actually started with this approach - and an even smaller number have made serious progress at this point. The organization change projects that were thought to be necessary to convert to a process-focused organization were not all successful.

These findings lead us to conclude that the majority of organizations in the world require access to good information and best practices concerning the **business processes of**

IT organizations. Fortunately, that information is abundant. The ITIL version 2 books provide comprehensive documentation on the most important processes, while ITIL version 3 adds even more information.

The **process model** is at least as important as the processes because processes must be deployed in the right relationships to achieve the desired effect of a process-focused approach. There are many different process models available. The experiences gained with these processes and process models in recent years have been documented comprehensively in books, magazines and white papers, and have been presented at countless conventions.

4.2 Management of processes

Every organization aims to realize its vision, mission, strategy, objectives and policies, which means that appropriate activities have to be undertaken.

For example, a restaurant will have to purchase fresh ingredients, the chefs will have to work together to provide consistent results, and there should be no major differences in style among the waiting staff. A restaurant will only be awarded a three-star rating when it manages to provide the same high quality over an extended period of time. This is not always the case: there will be changes among the waiting staff, a successful approach may not last, and chefs often leave to open their own restaurants. Providing consistently high quality means that the component activities have to be coordinated: the better and more efficiently the kitchen operates, the higher the quality of service that can be provided to the guests.

In the example of the restaurant, appropriate activities include buying vegetables, bookkeeping, ordering publicity material, receiving guests, cleaning tables, peeling potatoes and making coffee. With just such an unstructured list, something will be left out and staff will easily become confused. It is therefore a better idea to structure the activities. Preferably these will be structured in such a way as to allow us to see how each group of activities contributes to the objectives of the business, and how they are related to other activities.

Such groups of activities are known as **processes**. If the process structure of an organization is clearly described, it will show:
- what has to be done
- what the expected inputs and results are

- how we measure whether the processes deliver the expected results
- how the results of one process affect those of another process

Processes can be defined in many ways. Depending upon the objectives of the creator, more or less emphasis will be on specific aspects. For example, a highly detailed process description will allow for a high level of control. Superficial process definitions will illustrate that the creator does not care much about the way in which the steps are executed.

Once the processes are defined, the roles, responsibilities and people can be assigned to specific aspects, bringing the process to the level of a *procedure*.

Processes

When arranging activities into processes, we do not use the existing allocation of tasks, nor the existing departmental divisions. This is a conscious choice. By opting for a process structure, it often becomes evident that certain activities in the organization are uncoordinated, duplicated, neglected or unnecessary.

> A *process* is a structured set of activities designed to accomplish a defined objective.

Instead, we look at the **objective** of the process and the **relationships** with other processes. A process is a series of activities carried out to convert input into an output, and ultimately into an outcome. The **input** is concerned with the resources being used in the process. The (reported) **output** describes the immediate results of the process, while the **outcome** indicates the long-term results of the process (in terms of meaningful effect). Through **control** activities, we can associate the input and output of each of the processes with **policies and standards** to provide information about the results to be obtained by the process. Control regulates the input and the **throughput** in case the throughput or output parameters are not compliant with these standards and policies. This produces chains of processes that show the input that goes into the organization and what the result, and it also monitors points in the chains in order to check the quality of the products and services provided by the organization.

The standards for the output of each process have to be defined, in such a way that the complete chain of processes in the process model meets the corporate objective. If the output of a process meets the defined requirements, then the process is **effective** in transforming its input into its output. To be really effective, the outcome should be taken into consideration rather than merely focusing on the output. If the activities in the process are also carried out with the minimum required effort and cost, then the process is **efficient**. It is the task of process management to use **planning and control** to ensure that processes are executed in an effective and efficient way.

We can study each process separately to optimize its quality. The **process owner** is responsible for the process results. The **process manager** is responsible for the realization and structure of the process, and reports to the process owner.

The logical combination of activities results in clear transfer points where the quality of processes can be monitored. In the restaurant example, we can separate responsibility for purchasing and cooking, so that the chefs do not have to purchase anything and can concentrate on their core activities.

The management of the organization can provide control on the basis of the process quality of the process as demonstrated by data from the results of each process. In most cases, the relevant **performance indicators** and standards will already be agreed upon. In this case the process manager can do the day-to-day control of the process. The process owner will assess the results based on a **report** of performance indicators and checks whether the results meet the agreed standard. Without clear indicators, it would be difficult for a process owner to determine whether the process is under control, and if planned improvements are being implemented.

Processes are often described using **procedures** and **work instructions**.

> A **procedure** is a specified way to carry out an activity or a process. A procedure describes the "how", and can also describe "who" carries the activities out. A procedure may include stages from different processes. A procedure can vary depending on the organization.
>
> A set of **work instructions** defines how one or more activities in a procedure should be carried out in detail, using technology or other resources.

A process is defined as a logically related series of activities executed to meet the goals of a defined objective. Processes are composed of two kinds of activities: the activities to realize the goal (operational activities concerned with the throughput), and the activities to manage these (control activities). The control activities make sure the operational activities (the workflow) are performed in time, in the right order, etc. (For example, in the processing of changes it is always ensured that a test is performed *before* a release is taken into production and not *afterwards*.)

Processes and departments

Most businesses are hierarchically organized. There are departments that are responsible for the activities of a group of employees. There are various ways of structuring departments, such as by customer, product, region or discipline. IT services generally depend on several departments, customers or disciplines. For example, if there is an IT service to provide users with access to an accounting program on a central computer, this will involve several disciplines. The computer center has to make the program and database accessible, the data and telecommunications department has to make the computer center accessible, and the PC support team has to provide users with an interface to access the application.

Processes that span several departments (teams) can monitor the quality of a service by monitoring particular aspects of quality, such as availability, capacity, cost and stability. A service organization will try to match these quality aspects with the customer's demands. The structure of such processes can ensure that good information is available about the provision of services, so that the planning and control of services can be improved.

Figure 4.1 shows a basic example of the combinations of activities in a process (indicated by the dashed lines).

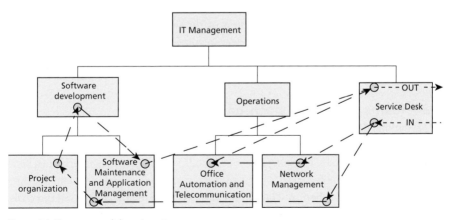

Figure 4.1 Processes and departments

IT service management and processes

IT service management has been known as the process and service-focused approach of what was initially known as Information Technology management. The shift of management from infrastructure to processes has paved the way for the term IT service management as a process and customer-focused discipline. Processes should always have a defined objective. The objective of IT service management processes is to contribute to the quality of the IT services. Quality management and process control are part of the organization and its policies.

By using a process approach, best practices for IT service management describe how services can be delivered, using the most effective and efficient series of activities. The Service Lifecycle in ITIL V3 is based on these process descriptions. The structure and allocation of tasks and responsibilities between functions and departments depends on the type of organization, and these structures vary widely among IT departments, and they often change. The description of the process structure however, provides a common point of reference that changes less rapidly. This can help to maintain the quality of IT services during and after reorganizations, and also among service providers and partners as they change. This makes service providers far less sensitive to organizational change, and much more flexible: providers can continually adapt their organization to changing conditions, leaving the core of their processes in place. In this way the shop can stay open during reconstruction work. However, reality may pose some practical problems, making this more difficult in practice than it seems in theory.

Applying the best process definitions of the industry allows IT service providers to concentrate on their business. As with other fields of industry, the processes in the IT industry are similar for all organizations of the same nature. Many of the process descriptions documented in ITIL have been recognized as the best that the industry could hope to adopt.

4.3   Teams, roles and positions in ITSM

Organizations divide the various tasks for carrying out processes or activities in many different ways. Tasks can be covered by organizational bodies, such as groups, teams, departments or divisions. These organizational bodies are then managed in **hierarchical organizations** by a line manager, who has a certain "span of control" and who manages one or more of these bodies. **Flat organizations** have relatively few layers in this hierarchy. Organizations can also divide the tasks more in the spirit of equality, such as, for example, **network organizations**, in which the cooperation between the various bodies is paramount.

Besides hierarchical organizations, which manage through "the line", there are also **project organizations**, which manage primarily by using temporary forms of project cooperation, while **process organizations** are managed primarily by means of an agreed work method. Obviously, these types of management can be combined in innumerable ways. As a result of this, we are seeing a great number of unique organizational configurations in the field.

Organizations can distinguish themselves from other organizations, particularly in respect to the type of organization they operate. An organization that is directed toward hierarchy will have a staff primarily of senior line management. A process-oriented organization will have staff that are responsible for processes. Depending on the degree to which management is based on processes, the line or projects, the staff will consist of a mix of the relevant responsible managers.

When setting up an organization, positions and roles are also used, in addition to the various groups (teams, departments, divisions). **Roles** are sets of responsibilities, activities and authorities granted to a person or team. One person or team may have multiple roles; for example, the roles of Configuration Manager and Change Manager may be carried out by a single person. **Positions** (functions) are traditionally recognized as tasks and responsibilities that are assigned to a specific person. A person in a particular position has a clearly defined package of tasks and responsibilities which may include various roles. Positions can also be more broadly defined as a logical concept that refers to the people and automated measures that carry out a clearly defined process, an activity or a combination of processes or activities.

4.4 Tools used in ITSM

In the performance of tasks in IT service management, innumerable automated support aids can be used: these are referred to as tools. With the help of these tools, management tasks can be automated; for example, monitoring tasks or software distribution tasks. Other tools support the performance of the activities themselves; for example, service desk tools or service management tools. The latter category, in fact, supports the management of several processes and are therefore often referred to as workflow tools - although they may not have actual workflow engines.

The fact that the IT field is fundamentally focused on automated facilities (for information processing) has led to a virtual deluge of tools appearing on the market, which have greatly increased the performance capacity of IT organizations.

4.5   Communication in IT service organizations

People, process, partners and technology provide the main "machinery" of any organization, but they only work well if the machine is oiled: **communication** is an essential element in any organization. If the people do not know about the processes or use the wrong instructions or tools, the output may not be as anticipated.

People are core assets of the organization. This is not only due to the fact that they need to be in place to perform certain activities or to take decisions, but also because people have the good habit of communicating. When an organization applies highly detailed instructions for all its activities, it will end up in a bureaucracy. On the other hand, an organization without any rules is will most likely end up in chaos. Whichever balance an organization is trying to find here, it will always benefit enormously from communication between the people in the organization. A regular and formal meeting culture will support this, but organizations should not underestimate the important role of informal communication: many projects have been saved by means of a simple chat in the tea room, or in the car park.

Formal structures on communication include:
- **reporting** - internal and external reporting, aimed at management or customers, project progress reports, alerts
- **meetings** - formal project meetings, regular meetings with specific targets
- **online facilities** - email systems, chat-rooms, pagers, groupware, document sharing systems, messenger facilities, teleconferencing and virtual meeting facilities
- **notice boards** - near the coffee maker, water cooler, at the entrance of the building, in the company restaurant

IT teams and departments, as well as users, internal customers and service production teams, must communicate with each other. The **stakeholders** for communication can thus be found among all managers and employees who are involved in service management, in all the layers of the organization, and with all customers, users and service providers. Good communication can prevent problems. All communication must have a particular goal or result. Every team, process and every department must have a clear **communications policy**.

IT service management includes several types of communication, such as:
- routine operational communication
- communication between teams
- performance reports
- communication during projects

- communication when there are changes
- communication in case of exceptions
- communication in case of emergencies
- training for new or adapted processes and service designs
- communication with service production teams regarding service strategies and design

4.6 Culture

Organizations that want to change, for example to improve the quality of their services, will eventually be confronted with the current organizational culture and will have to deal with any changes to this culture as a consequence of the overall change. The organizational culture, or corporate culture, refers to the way in which people deal with each other in the organization; the way in which decisions are made and implemented; and the attitude of employees to their work, customers, service providers, superiors and colleagues.

Culture, which depends on the standards and values of the people in the organization, cannot be controlled, but it can be influenced. Influencing the culture of an organization requires leadership in the form of a clear and consistent policy, as well as a supportive personnel policy.

The corporate culture can have a major influence on the provision of IT services. Businesses value innovation in different ways. In a stable organization, where the culture places little value on innovation, it will be difficult to adjust its IT services in line with changes in the organization of the customer. If the IT department is unstable, then a culture which values change can pose a serious threat to the quality of its services. In that case, a "free for all" culture can develop where many uncontrolled changes lead to a large number of faults.

4.7 Processes, projects, programs and portfolios

Activities can be managed from a process perspective, from an organizational hierarchy (line) perspective, from a project perspective, or from any combination of these three. Organizations that tend to apply just one of these management systems often miss the benefits of the others. The practical choice often depends upon history, culture, available skills and competences, and personal preferences. The optimum choice may be entirely different, but the requirements for applying this optimum may be hard to realize and vary in time.

There are no "hard and fast laws" for the way an organization should combine processes, projects and programs. However, it is generally accepted that there are some consequences attached to modern practices in IT service organizations, since the most widely accepted approach to service management is based on process management. This means that whenever the organization works with projects or programs, it should have established how these approaches work together.

The practical relationship between projects and processes is determined by the relative position of both in terms of "leading principles for the management of the organization": if projects are considered more important than processes, then decisions on projects will overrule decisions on processes; as a consequence, the organization will not be able to implement a stable set of processes. If it is the other way around, with projects only able to run within the constraints of agreed processes, then project management will be a discipline that will have to adapt to new boundaries and definitions (e.g. since projects always change something from A to B, they will most likely fall under the regime of Change, Release and Deployment Management).

The most suitable solution is dependent upon the understanding of the role of IT service management in the organization. To be able to find a solution for this management challenge, it is recommended that a common understanding of processes, projects, programs, and even portfolio's is created. The following definitions may be used:

- **Process** - A process is a structured set of activities designed to accomplish a defined objective.
- **Project** - A project is a temporary organization, with people and other assets required to achieve an objective.
- **Program** - A program consists of a number of projects and activities that are planned and managed together to achieve an overall set of related objectives.
- **Portfolio** - A portfolio is a set of projects and/or programs, which are not necessarily related, brought together for the sake of control, coordination and optimization of the portfolio in its totality. NB: In ITIL, a service portfolio is the complete set of services that are managed by a service provider.

Since the project/program/portfolio grouping is a hierarchical set of essential project resources, the issue can be downscaled to that of a relationship between a project and a process.

The most elementary difference between a process and a project is the one-off character of a project, versus the continuous character of the process. If a project has achieved its objectives, it means the end of the project. Processes can be run many times, both in parallel and in sequence. The nature of a process is aimed at its repeatable character:

processes are defined only in case of a repeatable string of activities that are important enough to be standardized and optimized.

Projects are aimed at changing a situation A into a situation B. This can involve a simple string of activities, but it can also be a very complex series of activities. Other elements of importance for projects include money, time, quality, organization and information. Project structures are normally used only if at least one of these elements is of considerable value.

Actually, projects are just ways of organizing a specific change in a situation. In that respect they have a resemblance with processes. It is often a matter of focus: processes focus at the specific sequence of activities, the decisions taken at certain milestone stages, and the quality of the activities involved. Processes are continuously instantiated and repeated, and use the same approach each time. Projects focus more at the time and money constraints, in terms of resources spent on the change and the projects end, and projects vary much more than processes.

A very practical way of combining the benefits of both management systems might be as follows:

- Processes set the scene for how specific series of activities are performed.
- Projects can be used to transform situation A into situation B, and always refer to a change.
- If the resources (time, money, or other) involved in a specific process require the level of attention that is normally applied in a project, then (part of) the process activities can be performed as a project, but always under the control of the process: if changes are performed, using project management techniques, the agreed change management policies still apply.

This would allow organizations to maintain a continuous customer focus and apply a process approach to optimize this customer focus, and at the same time benefit from the high level of resource control that can be achieved when using project management techniques.

4.8 Functions and processes in the lifecycle phases

For the sake of readability and uniformity, the following structure for the descriptions was used as much as possible:

- **introduction** - describes the purpose and aims of the process or function, its scope, value to the business, principles, guidelines, starting points and basic concepts

- **activities, methods and techniques** - explains the process or function in greater detail based on the workflow of activities (if possible); also describes commonly used methods and techniques
- **interfaces** - describes how the process or function is triggered, its inputs and outputs, and its links to other functions and processes
- **metrics** - describes the process metrics, in particular the Key Performance Indicators (KPIs)
- **implementation** - describes the Critical Success Factors (CSFs), challenges, risks and traps that may apply for the introduction of a process or function

CHAPTER 5

Functions and Processes in Service Operation

5.1 Event Management

Introduction

ITIL defines an event as follows:

> An **event** can be defined as any detectable or discernible occurrence that has significance for the management of the IT infrastructure or the delivery of IT service and evaluation of the impact a deviation may cause to the services.

Events are typically notifications created by an IT service, CI or monitoring tool. To ensure effective Service Operations, an organization must be aware of the status of its infrastructure and be able to detect deviations from the regular or expected operation. Good monitoring and control systems are required.

The **objective** of event management is to detect events, analyze them and determine the right management action. It provides the entry point for the execution of many Service Operation processes and activities.

Scope

Event management can be applied to any aspect of service management that requires control and can be automated. For example configuration items, security, software license monitoring and environmental conditions (e.g. detecting fire and smoke).

Value for the business

Event management generally has indirect value. Some examples of added value for the business:

- event management provides mechanisms for early detection of incidents
- event management makes it possible for some types of automated activity to be monitored by exception
- if event management is integrated into other service management processes, it may detect status changes or exceptions; this allows the right person or team to respond more quickly, thereby improving the process performance
- event management provides a basis for automated operations; this improves effectiveness and frees up costly human resources for more innovative work

Basic concepts

There are many different event types, such as:

- events that indicate a normal operation, such as a user logging on to use an application
- events that indicate an exception, such as a user who is trying to log on to an application with an incorrect password or a PC scan that reveals the installation of unauthorized software
- events that signify an unusual but not exceptional operation; it may provide an indication that the situation requires a little more supervision For example utilization of a server's memory reaches within five per cent of its highest acceptable level

Activities, methods and techniques

The diagram in Figure 5.1 reflects the flow of event management. It is a high level and generic representation and should be used as a reference point rather than an actual event management flowchart.

The main activities of the event management process are:

- **an event occurs** - events occur all the time, but they are not all detected or registered; it is therefore important for everyone who develops, designs, manages and supports IT services and IT infrastructure to understand what event types must be detected
- **event reporting** - most CIs are designed in such a way that they communicate specific information about themselves in one of the following ways:
  - a management tool probes a device and collects specific data; this is also called "polling"
  - the CI generates a report if certain conditions are met
- **event detection** - a management tool or agent detects an event report and reads and interprets it

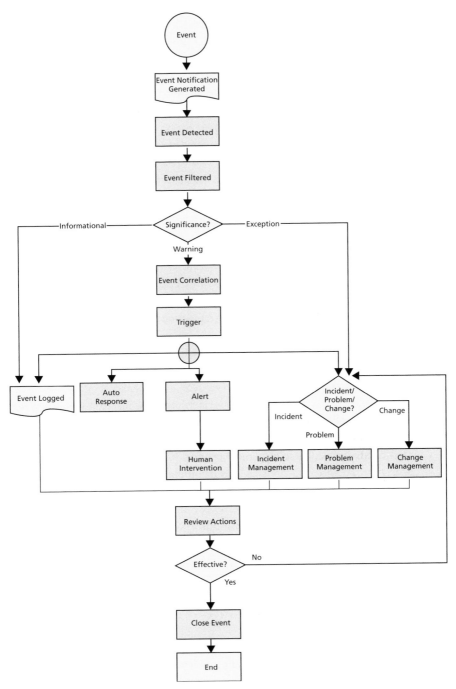

Figure 5.1 Event management

- **event filtering** - decides whether or not the event is communicated to a management tool; if not, the device registers the event in a log file and refrains from taking any further action
- **the significance of events (event classification)** - an organization often uses its own classification to establish the importance of an event, but it is useful to use at least the following three broad categories:
  - *informative* - an event that does not require action and is not an exception, e.g. a user logging into an application; is generally stored in the system or service log files and saved for a certain period
  - *alert* - occurs when a service or device reaches a threshold; warns the specified person, process or tool to enable it to bring the situation under control and take the required action to prevent an exception; an example of an alert: memory capacity usage on a server is currently at 65% and increasing; if it reaches 75%, the response times are too long and it exceeds the OLA
  - *Exception* - means that a service or device is behaving abnormally and a failure to comply with an OLA or SLA; examples of exceptions are:
    - a server is down
    - the response time of a standard transaction over a network exceeds 15 seconds
    - part of the network does not respond to routine queries
- **event correlation** - establishes the significance of an event and determines what actions should be taken
- **trigger** - if the event is recognized a response is required; the mechanism that initiates that response is called a *trigger*; there are different trigger types, including:
  - *incident triggers* generate a record in the incident management system, thereby starting up the incident management process
  - *scripts* execute specific actions, such as rebooting a device
  - *database triggers* deny a user access to specific records or fields, or create and delete entries in a database
- **response options** - the process provides a number of response options, a combination of which are allowed:
  - event logging
  - automatic response
  - alert and human intervention
  - submitting a *Request for Change (RFC)*
  - opening an incident record
  - open or link to a problem record
- **reviewing actions** - thousands of events are generated every day, which makes it impossible to assess each individual event formally; however, you should check all

important events or exceptions to determine whether they have been treated correctly, or whether event types are counted; in many cases this can be done automatically
- **closing the event** - some events remain open until specific actions have been taken, e.g. an event linked to an open incident. However most events are not "opened" or "closed".

Interfaces
Any type of occurrence can **trigger** event management. The key is to determine what events are important and require action. Triggers include:
- exceptions at any level of CI performance defined in the design specifications, Operational Level Agreements or standard processing procedures
- an exception in a business process that is monitored by event management
- a status change in a device or database record
- completion of an automated task or job
- access of an application or database by a user

Event management can **interface** to any process that requires monitoring and control. The most important are incident, problem and change management. In addition, configuration management can use events to determine the current status of a CI in the infrastructure. Events represent a rich source of information for knowledge management systems.

Metrics
Metrics are required for every measuring period, to verify the effectiveness and efficiency of the event management process, e.g.
- number of events by category
- number of events by significance
- number and percentage of events requiring human intervention and whether this was performed
- the number and percentage of events that resulted in incidents or changes
- the number and percentage of each event type per platform or application

Implementation
The main **risks** are:
- being unable to realize sufficient funds
- establishing the right level of filtering
- being unable to maintain momentum during rollout of the required *monitoring agents*

Designing for event management

Event management is the basis for monitoring the performance and availability of a service. This is why availability and capacity management must specify and agree on the precise monitoring targets and mechanisms. Various instruments exist for this purpose:

- **instrumentation** - defines how best to monitor and manage the IT infrastructure and IT services, and creates an appropriate design.

  Determine:
  - what needs to be monitored
  - what monitoring type is required (active or passive, performance or output)
  - when the monitoring should generate an event
  - what type of information needs to be communicated
  - who is the audience

  Mechanisms that need to be designed include:
  - how will events be generated
  - does the CI already have event generation
  - what data will be used to populate the event record
  - are events generated automatically or does the CI have to be polled
  - where will events be logged and stored

- **error messages** - important for all components (hardware, software, networks, etc); design all software applications in such a way that they can support event management, e.g. by means of meaningful error messages or codes that clearly indicate what is going wrong, where and the likely causes

- **event detection and alert mechanisms** - for a good design, you need the following:
  - detailed knowledge of the Service Level Requirements of the service that is supported by every CI
  - information on who will support the CI
  - knowledge of the normal and abnormal state of affairs for the CI
  - information that can help determine problems with CIs

5.2 Incident Management

Introduction

The incident management process handles all incidents. These may be failures, questions or queries that are reported by users (generally via a call to the service desk) or technical staff, or that are automatically detected and reported by tools to monitor events.

ITIL defines an incident as:

> An **incident** is an unplanned interruption to an IT service or reduction in the quality of an IT service. Failure of a CI that has not yet affected service is also an incident.

The main **objective** of the incident management process is to resume the regular state of affairs as quickly as possible and minimize the impact on business processes.

Scope

Incident management covers every event that disrupts or might disrupt a service. This means that it includes events reported directly by users, either via the service desk or various tools.

Incidents can also be reported or logged by technical staff, which does not necessarily mean that every event is an incident.

While incidents and *service requests* are both reported to the service desk, they are not the same thing. *service requests* are not service disruptions but user requests for support, delivery, information, advice or documentation.

Value for the business

The value of incident management includes:
- the possibility to track and solve incidents results in reduced downtime for the business; as a result the service is available for longer
- the possibility to align IT operations with the business priorities; the reason is that incident management is able to identify business priorities and distribute resources dynamically
- the possibility to establish potential improvements for services

Incident management is clearly visible to the business, meaning that its value is easier to demonstrate than for other areas in Service Operations. For this reason, it is one of the first processes to be implemented in service management projects.

Basic concepts

The following elements should be taken into account in incident management:

- **Time limits** - Agree on time limits for all phases and use them as targets in Operational Level Agreements (OLAs) and Underpinning Contracts (UCs).
- **Incident models** - An incident model is a way to determine the steps that are necessary to execute a process correctly (in this case, the processing of certain incident types); it means that standard incidents will be handled correctly and within the agreed timeframes.
- **Major incidents** - A separate procedure is required for major incidents, with shorter timeframes and higher urgency; agree what a major incident is and map the entire incident priority system.

People sometimes confuse a major incident with a problem. However, an incident always remains an incident. Its impact or priority may increase, but it never becomes a problem. A problem is the underlying cause of one or more incidents and always remains a separate entity.

Activities, methods and techniques

The incident management process consists of the following steps (Figure 5.2):

1. identification
2. registration
3. classification
4. prioritization
5. diagnosis
6. escalation
7. investigation and diagnosis
8. resolution and recovery
9. closing

An incident is not handled until it is known to exist. This is called **incident identification**. From a business perspective, it is generally unacceptable to wait until a user experiences the impact of an incident and contacts the service desk. The organization must try to monitor all important components, so that failures or potential failures can be detected as early as possible and the incident management process can be initiated. In the perfect situation, incidents are solved before they have an impact on the users.

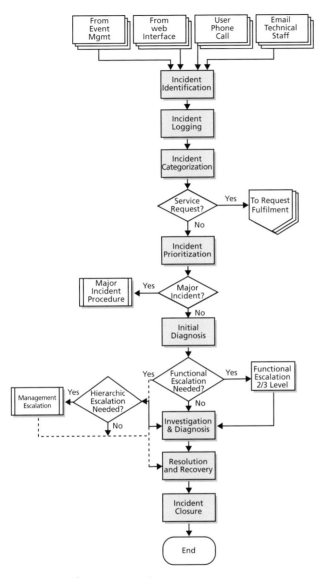

Figure 5.2 Incident management

All incidents must be registered in full, including date and time: **incident registration**. This applies to incidents received via the service desk as well as those that are detected automatically via an event warning system. Register all relevant information relating to the nature of the incident to ensure a complete historical record. If the incident is

transferred to other support groups, they will have all of the relevant information at their disposal. You should at least record:
- a unique reference number
- incident category
- incident urgency
- incident priority
- name/ID of the person and/or group who registered the incident
- description of symptoms
- activities undertaken to solve the incident

Use an appropriate **incident classification** coding for registration to record the precise call type. This is important at a later stage when incident types and frequencies are analyzed, to establish trends that can be used for problem management, provider management and other ITSM activities.

When registering an incident, it is possible that the available data are incomplete, misleading or incorrect. It is therefore important to check the classification of the incident and update it while concluding a call. An example of a categorized incident is: software, application, finance suite and purchase order system.

Another important aspect of registering every incident is to allocate the right **priority** code. Support agents and tools use this code to determine how they should handle the incident.

The priority of an incident can usually be determined by establishing its urgency (how fast does the business need a solution) and impact. The number of users touched by an incident is often an indication of its impact.

When a user reports an incident via the service desk, the service desk agent must try to record the greatest possible number of symptoms of the incident in terms of a first **diagnosis**. He also tries to establish what went wrong and how it should be corrected. Diagnostic scripts and *known error* information can be very useful in this context. If possible, the help desk agent solves the incident immediately and closes the incident. If this is impossible, the incident is *escalated*.

This can be achieved in two ways:
- **Functional escalation** - If it is clear that the service desk cannot solve the incident (quickly enough), it must be escalated immediately for further support; if the organization has a second line support group and the service desk believes that they can solve the incident, it forwards the incident to the second line; if it is clear that more technical knowledge is required for the incident and the second line support is

unable to solve the incident within the agreed timeframe, it must be escalated to the third line support group.

- **Hierarchical escalation** - The relevant IT managers must be warned in the event of more serious incidents (e.g. priority 1 incidents); hierarchical escalation is also used if there are inadequate resources to solve the incident; hierarchical escalation means that the organization calls upon the management higher up in the chain; senior managers are aware of the incident and can take the required steps, such as allocating additional resources or calling upon suppliers.

When handling an incident, each support group **investigates** what went wrong. It also makes a **diagnosis**. Document all these activities in the incident record to ensure that a complete overview of all activities is available.

In case of incidents where the user is only looking for information, the service desk must be able to provide the answer quickly and solve the *service request*.

If a possible solution has been determined, it must be implemented and tested: Solution and recovery. The following actions can then be taken:

- ask the user to perform specific operations on his desktop
- the service desk can execute the solution centrally or use remote software to take control of the user's computer and implement a solution
- ask a supplier to solve the error

The support group returns the incident to the service desk, which **closes the incident**. However, it first checks that the incident has been solved and that the users are satisfied with the solution. It must also close the classification, check that the user is satisfied, update the incident documentation, determine whether the incident could recur, and decide whether action should be taken to prevent this. The incident can then be formally closed.

Information management

Most information used by incident management is provided by incident management tools and incident records. Incident management also has access to the Configuration Management System (CMS). This makes it possible to identify the CIs touched by the incident. The impact of the incident can also be assessed.

Interfaces

Incidents can be **triggered** in many ways. The most common route is via a user who calls the service desk or completes an incident registration form via the internet. However, many incidents are registered more and more often by event management tools.

The processes below have **interfaces** with incident management:

- **Problem management** - Incidents are often caused by underlying problems that must be solved to prevent the incident from recurring. Incident management offers a place to report these problems.
- **Configuration management** - Configuration management provides the data used to identify and track incidents. The configuration management system (CMS) is used, among other things, to identify defective components and determine the impact of an incident. The CMS is also used to identify the users who are impacted by potential problems.
- **Change management** - If a change is necessary to implement a workaround or solution, it is registered as an RFC and executed by change management. Incident management is able to track and solve incidents resulting from inappropriate changes.
- **Capacity management** - Incident management triggers performance monitoring if a performance problem occurs. Capacity management can offer workarounds for incidents.
- **Availability management** - Availability management uses data from incident management to determine the availability of IT services, and establishes where the incident lifecycle can be improved.
- **Service Level Management (SLM)** - SLM monitors the agreements with customers concerning the support to be provided. Incident management reports to SLM. This process, for instance, can evaluate SLAs objectively and regularly. SLM establish acceptable service levels within which incident management must work.

Metrics

Metrics make it possible to assess the effectiveness, efficiency and operation of the incident management process. Examples of metrics are:

- the total number of incidents
- the number and percentage of major incidents
- the average cost per incident
- the number and percentage of incorrectly allocated incidents
- the percentage of incidents handled within the agreed timeframe

Implementation

Incident management has the following **challenges**:

- to detect incidents as quickly as possible
- to convince all staff (both technical teams and users) that all incidents must be registered and encourage them to use web-based options to solve incidents themselves

- the availability of information about problems and known errors, enabling incident management staff to learn from previous incidents and track the status of solutions
- integration with the configuration management system to determine the relationship between CIs and refer to the history of CIs when providing first line support
- integration with the service level management process; this helps incident management to determine the impact and priority of incidents correctly and to define and execute escalation procedures

The following **Critical Success Factors** (CSFs) are vital to successful incident management:
- a good service desk
- clearly defined SLA targets
- adequate support staff that is customer-oriented and technically qualified, and possesses the right competencies at all process levels
- integrated support tools to control and manage the process
- OLAs and UCs to influence and shape the behavior of all support personnel

Risks for successful incident management are:
- being overwhelmed by incidents that cannot be handled within an acceptable timeframe due to lack of well-trained resources
- incidents that make no progress because inadequate support tools fail to give warning or report progress
- lack of adequate information sources due to unsuitable tools or lack of integration
- no coinciding objectives or actions due to unaligned or nonexistent OLAs or UCs

5.3   Request Fulfilment

Introduction

ITIL uses the term service request as a general description for the varying requests that users submit to the IT department.

> A **service request** is a request from a user for information, advice, a standard change, or access to a service.

For example, a service request can be a request for a password change or the additional installation of a software application on a certain work station. Because these requests occur on a regular basis and involve little risk, it is better that they are handled in a separate process.

Request fulfilment (implementation of requests) processes service requests from the users. The **objectives** of the request fulfilment process are:

- to offer users a channel through which they can request and receive services; to this effect an agreed approval and qualification process must exist
- to provide users and customers with information about the availability of services and the procedure for obtaining these services
- to supply the components of standard services (for instance, licenses and software media)
- to assist with general information, complaints or comments

Scope

The process for handling requests depends on the nature of the request. In most cases the process can be divided into a series of activities that need to be completed. Some organizations treat the service requests as a special type of incident. However, there is an important difference between an incident and a service request. An incident is usually an unplanned event, whereas a service request tends to be something that can and must be planned.

Value for the business

The value of request fulfilment is the ability to offer fast and effective access to standard services that the business can use to improve the productivity or the quality of the business services and products.

Request fulfilment reduces the amount of "red tape" in requesting and receiving access to existing or new services. This reduces the cost for the supply of these services.

Basic concepts
Many service requests recur on a regular basis. This is why a process flow can be devised in advance, stipulating the phases needed to handle the requests, the individuals or support groups involved, time limits and escalation paths. The service request is usually handled as a standard change.

Activities, working methods and techniques
Request fulfilment consists of the following activities, methods and techniques:
- **menu selection** - by means of request fulfilment, users can submit their own service request via a link to service management tools; in the ideal situation the user will be offered a menu via a web interface, so that they can select and enter the details of a service request
- **financial approval** - most service requests have financial implications; the cost for handling a request must first be determined; it is possible to agree fixed prices for standard requests and give instant authorization for these requests; in all other cases the cost must first be estimated, after which the user must give permission
- **fulfillment** - the actual fulfillment activity depends on the nature of the service request; the service desk can handle simple requests, whereas others must be forwarded to specialist groups or suppliers
- **closure** - once the service request has been completed the service desk will close off the request

Interfaces
Most requests are **triggered** by a user who rings the service desk or a user who completes a request form on-screen. Many service requests come in via the service desks and can be handled through the incident management process. Some organizations choose to handle all requests via this route, others prefer a separate process.

There is also a strong **link** between request fulfillment, release management, asset management and configuration management, because some requests deal with the roll-out of new or improved components that can be implemented automatically.

Request fulfilment is dependent on information from the following **sources**:
- service requests
- Requests for Change

- service portfolio
- security policy

Metrics

The metrics required to evaluate the efficiency and effectiveness of request fulfilment are:
- the total number of service requests
- the breakdown of service requests by phase
- the size of the current backlog of outstanding service requests
- the average time for handling each type of service request
- the number and percentage of service requests that are handled within the agreed time
- the average cost per type of service request
- the level of customer satisfaction in respect of the handling of service requests

Implementation

Request fulfilment is faced with the following **challenges**:
- to clearly define and document the type of request that is being handled in the request fulfilment process, so that all parties know what the scope is
- to establish front-end options, so that users can make their own link to the request fulfilment process

Request fulfilment is dependent on the following **critical success factors**:
- there must be agreement about which services are standardized and who is authorized to request them; there must also be agreement about the cost of these services
- publication of these services for the benefit of the users, as part of the service catalogue
- there must be a definition of a standard fulfillment procedure for each service being requested
- there must be a <u>single</u> point of contact for requesting the service; this is often done via the service desk or via an internet request, but can also be made via an automated request directly in the request fulfilment procurement system
- self-service tools are needed to offer a front-end interface to users; it is important that this interface can communicate with the back-end fulfillment tools

Request fulfilment has the following **risks**:
- If the scope is ill-defined, people will not know exactly what the process is supposed to handle.

- Poorly designed or implemented user interfaces may make it difficult for users to submit requests.
- Poorly designed or realized back-end fulfillment processes may result in the system being unable to handle the number or type of requests being submitted.
- Insufficient monitoring capacity may result in no accurate metrics being collected.

5.4   Problem Management

Introduction
ITIL defines a problem as follows:

> A **problem** is the cause of one or more incidents.

Problem management is responsible for the control of the lifecycle of all problems. The primary **objective** of problem management is to prevent problems and incidents, eliminate repeating incidents and minimize the impact of incidents that cannot be prevented.

Scope
Problem management comprises all the activities needed to diagnose the underlying cause of incidents and to find a solution for these problems. It must also ensure that the solution is implemented via the correct control procedures, in other words through the use of change management and release management.

Value for the business
Problem management works together with incident management and change management to ensure improvements in the availability and quality of the IT service provision. When incidents are resolved the solution is registered. At a given moment this information is used to accelerate the incident handling and identify permanent solutions. This reduces the number of incidents and the handling time, resulting in shorter disruption times and fewer disruptions to the business critical systems.

Basic concepts
Many problems are unique and need to be handled separately. However, it is possible that some incidents may occur more than once as a result of underlying problems.

ITIL defines a known error as:

> A **known error** is a problem that has a documented root cause and a workaround.

ITIL defines a workaround as:

> **Workaround**: reducing or eliminating the impact of an incident or problem for which a full resolution is not yet available.

In addition to creating a Known Error Database (KEDB) for faster diagnoses, the creation of a **problem model** for the handling of future problems may be useful. Such a standard model supports with the steps that need to be taken, the responsibilities of people involved and the necessary timescales.

Activities, methods and techniques

Problem management consists of two important processes:
- **reactive problem management** - performed by Service Operation
- **proactive problem management** - initiated by Service Operation, but usually managed by CSI (Continual Service Improvement)

Reactive problem management consists of the following activities (Figure 5.3):
- identification
- registration
- classification
- prioritization
- investigation and diagnosis
- decide on workarounds
- identification of known errors
- resolution
- conclusion
- review
- correction of errors found

Identification of problems is carried out using the following methods:
- The service desk suspects or identifies an unknown cause of one or more incidents. This results in a problem registration. It may also be clear straightaway that an incident was caused by a major problem. In this case a problem registration takes place immediately.
- Analysis of an incident by the technical support group reveals that there is an underlying problem.
- There is automatic tracing of an infrastructural or application error, whereby event or alert tools automatically create an incident registration that highlights the need for a problem registration.
- The supplier reports a problem that needs to be resolved.

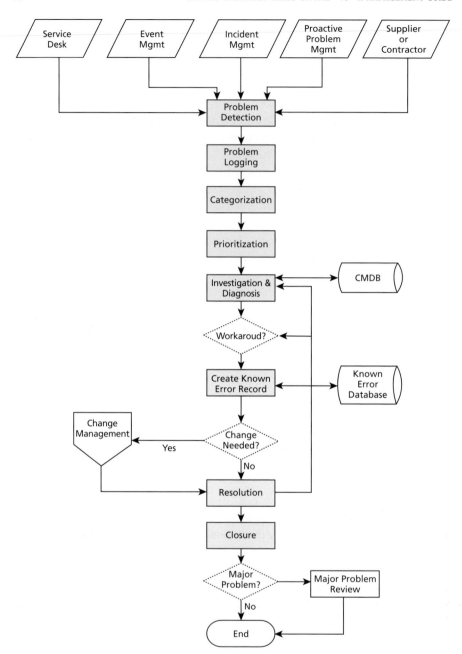

Figure 5.3 Problem management

- Analysis of incidents takes place as part of corrective problem management. This results in a problem registration so that the underlying cause can be investigated further.

Analyze incident and problem data on a regular basis in order to identify trends. To this effect an efficient and detailed classification of incidents and problems is required, as well as regular reporting of patterns and problem areas.

Irrespective of the identification method, all details of the problem must be registered (**problem registration**), so that a comprehensive historic report is created. The information must be date and time stamped, so that proper control and escalation are possible.

Problems must be classified in the same way as incidents, so that the true nature of the problem can be established quickly and easily. **Problem classification** provides useful management information.

As is the case for incidents, problems must also be given a **priority** in the same manner and for the same reasons. In this context also take into account the frequency and impact of the related incidents and the seriousness of the problems. Examples of such considerations are:
- Can the system be repaired or does it need to be replaced?
- What are the costs?
- How many people, and with what expertise are needed to resolve the problem?
- How much time is needed to resolve the problem?
- How big is the problem?

In order to find the underlying cause of the problem and make a **diagnosis**, an **investigation** must be performed. The speed and nature of this investigation depend on the impact, seriousness and urgency of the problem. Use the proper level of resources and expertise to find a solution.

It is often useful to reproduce the problem, so that it becomes clear what went wrong. Next you can use different methods to determine what the best solution is. This is best done by using a test system that reflects production.

Many problem analysis, diagnosis and solution techniques are available, including:
- chronological analysis
- Pain Value Analysis

- Kepner-Tregoe
- brainstorming
- Ishikawa diagrams
- Pareto analysis

In some cases a temporary solution, a **workaround**, is possible for incidents that were caused by a problem. It is important, however, that the problem reporting remains open and that the details about the workaround are included in the problem reporting.

As soon as the diagnosis has been made, and especially if a workaround has been found, the **identified known errors** must be listed in a known error report and placed in the Known Error Database. Should other incidents and problems occur they can be identified and the service can be resumed more quickly.

As soon as a **solution** has been found it should, ideally, be applied to resolve the problem. In reality, there are preventative measures to make sure that the solution does not cause further problems. If a change in functionality is needed a *Request for Change* is required that must follow the steps of the change management process.

If the change has been completed and successfully evaluated and the solution has been applied, the problem report can formerly be **closed off**, as can the related incident reports that are still outstanding. Remember to check whether the report contains a full description of all the events.

After every **major problem** a **review** must be performed to learn lessons for the future. In particular the review must assess:
- what went well
- what went wrong
- what can be done better in future
- how the same problem can be prevented from recurring
- whether a third party is responsible and whether any follow-up actions are needed

It is very rare that new applications, systems or software releases do not contain **errors**. In most cases a priority system is used during testing that removes the most serious errors, but it is possible that minor errors are not corrected.

Information management

The *CMS* contains details on all the components of the IT infrastructure and on the relationship between these components. It is a valuable source for problem diagnosis and for the evaluation of the impact of problems.

The purpose of a **Known Error Database** (KEDB) is to store knowledge about incidents and problems and how they were remedied, so that a quicker diagnosis and solution can be found if further incidents and problems occur.

The known error registration must contain the exact details about the error and the symptoms that occurred, together with the exact details of a workaround or solution that can be implemented to resume the service or resolve the problem.

It may be that there is no business case for a permanent solution for certain problems. For instance, if the problem does not cause serious disruptions, a workaround already exists and the costs of resolving the problem exceed the advantages of a permanent solution, problem management may decide to tolerate the problem.

Like the configuration management system (CMS), the KEDB is part of a larger Service Knowledge Management System (SKMS) (Figure 5.4).

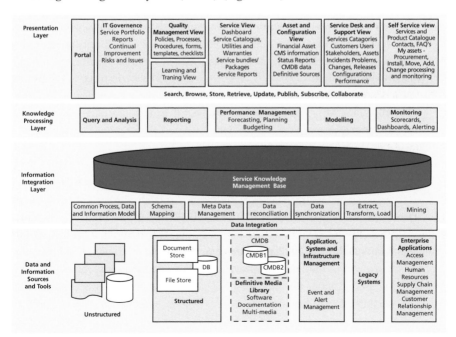

Figure 5.4 The Service Knowledge Management System

Interfaces

The majority of problem registrations are **triggered** as a response to one or more incidents, especially by service desk staff. Other problem registrations and corresponding known errors are triggered during testing, especially during so-called user acceptance tests that determine whether a release will proceed despite some known errors.

The following processes **interface** with problem management:

- **Service Transition**:
  - *change management* - problem management ensures that all solutions and workarounds for which change is necessary are implemented in a CI via an RFC; change management monitors the progress of these changes and keeps problem management informed
  - *configuration management* - problem management uses the CMS to identify wrong CIs and to determine the impact of problems and solutions
  - *release and deployment management* - is responsible for the rollout of problem fixes in a production environment
- **Service Design**:
  - *availability management* - helps determine how the disruption time can be minimized and how the production time (*uptime*) can be increased; a lot of the management information in problem management is passed on to availability management
  - *capacity management* - ensures the optimum use of resources and provides problem management with important information such as capacity registrations and performance matters; capacity management also supports the application of corrective measures
  - *IT Service Continuity Management (ITSCM)* - problem management acts as a starting point for ITSCM: a problem is not resolved if it does not have an important impact on the business
- **Continual Service Improvement**:
  - *service level management* - incidents and problems influence the quality of IT services provided by SLM; problem management contributes to improving service levels and the management information provided by it is used as the basis for some SLA review components
- **Service Strategy**:
  - *financial management* - problem management provides management information about the cost of resolving and preventing problems; in this way the information can be used as input for budgeting and accounting systems and Total Cost of Ownership calculations

Metrics

The following metrics are used to evaluate the efficiency, effectiveness and implementation of the problem management process:

- the total number of problems that were registered in the period
- the percentage of problems that were resolved within SLA targets (and the percentage of problems that were not solved)
- the number and percentage of problems for which more time was needed to resolve them
- the backlog of outstanding problems and the trend (static, decreasing, increasing)
- the average costs for handling a problem
- the number of major problems (outstanding, closed and backlog)
- the percentage of successful major problem reviews
- the number of known errors added to the KEDB
- the accuracy percentage of the KEDB (from checks of the database)

Implementation

Problem management is highly dependent on the formulation of an effective incident management process and the use of the proper tools. These help to identify problems as quickly as possible.

5.5   Access Management

Introduction

Access management grants authorized users the right to use a service, but denies unauthorized users access. Some organizations also call it "rights management" or "identity management".

Scope

Access management ensures that users have access to a service, but it does not guarantee that access is always available at the agreed times. This is handled by availability management.

Access management can be initiated via a number of mechanisms, such as the service desk by means of a *service request*.

Value for the business

Access management has the following value:
- controlled access to services enables the organization to maintain confidentiality of its information more effectively
- staff have the right access level to do their jobs properly
- the risk of errors during data entry or the use of a vital service by an unqualified user is lower
- there is the option to withdraw access rights more easily when it is necessary access may be necessary for compliance (e.g. SOX, HIPAA, CobiT)

Basic concepts

Access management has the following basic concepts:
- **access** - refers to the level and scope of the functionality of a service or data that a user is allowed to use
- **identity** - refers to the information about the persons who the organization distinguish as individuals; establishes their status in the organization
- **rights** (also called privileges) - refers to the actual settings for a user; which service (group) they are allowed to use; typical rights include reading, writing, executing, editing and deleting
- **services or service groups** - most users have access to multiple services; it is therefore more effective to grant every user or group of users access to an entire series of services that they are allowed to use simultaneously
- **directory services** - refers to a specific type of tool used to manage access and rights

Activities, methods and techniques

Access (or limitation of access) can be requested via a number of mechanisms, such as:
- a standard request generated by the human resources department; this generally occurs when someone is hired, promoted or leaves the company
- a *Request for Change (RFC)*
- an RFC submitted via the request fulfilment process
- execution of an authorized script or option

Access management consists of the following activities:
- **Verification** - Access management must verify every access request for an IT service from two perspectives:
  - Is the user requesting access truly the person he says he is?
  - Does the user have a legitimate reason to use the service?
- **Granting rights** - Access management does not decide who gets access to what IT services; it only executes the policy and rules defined by Service Strategy and Service Design.
  The more groups and roles exist, the greater the chance of a role conflict occurring. In this context, role conflicts refer to a situation in which two specific roles or groups allocated to a user can cause trouble due to conflicting interests. One example is that one role requires access while the other forbids it.
- **Monitoring identity status** - User roles may vary over time, with an impact on their service needs; examples of what may change a role are: job changes, promotion, dismissal, retirement or death.
- **Registering and monitoring access** - Access management does not only respond to requests; it must also ensure that the rights it has granted are used correctly.
  This is why access monitoring and control must be included in the monitoring activities of all technical and application management functions as well as all Service Operation processes.
- **Revoking or limiting rights** - In addition to granting rights to use a service, access management is also responsible for withdrawing those rights; but it cannot make the actual decision.

Information management

The **identity** of a user is the information that distinguishes him as an individual and verifies his status in the organization. The following data may be used, for instance:
- name
- contact details such as phone number and (e-mail) address
- physical documentation, such as driver's license and passport

- numbers referring to a document or entry in a database, such as social security number and driver's license number
- biometric information, such as fingerprints, DNA and voice recognition patterns

While every **user** has a separate identity and every IT service can be considered an individual identity, it often makes sense to **group** them for easier management. Sometimes the terms user profile, user template or **user role** are used to describe this type of grouping.

Most organizations have a standard collection of services for all individual users regardless of their position or job. But some users have a special role. For instance, in addition to the standard services a user may also fulfill a marketing management role for which he needs access to several special marketing and financial modeling tools and data.

Interfaces
Access management is **triggered** by a user's request for access to a service (group). Such a request may originate with:

- an RFC
- a service request
- a request from the Human Resources (HR) department
- a request from a manager or department fulfilling an HR role or who has made a decision to use a service for the first time

Access management has **relationships** with various other processes. Since every access request for a service represents a change, change management plays an important part in controlling the access requests.

Service level management monitors the agreements concerning access to each service. This includes the criteria for who has access to a service, the costs and the access level granted to different types of users.

Access management also has a close relationship with configuration management. The CMS can be used for data storage and be studied to determine the current access details.

Metrics
Metrics used to measure the effectiveness and efficiency of access management are:

- the number of access requests (*service requests* and RFCs)
- the number of times access has been granted by a service, user or department

- the number of incidents required to reset access rights
- the number of incidents caused by incorrect access settings

Implementation
The **conditions** for successful access management include:
- the possibility to verify a user's identity
- the possibility to verify the identity of the person or entity granting permission
- the possibility to grant several access rights to an individual user
- a database of all users and the rights they have been granted

5.6   Monitoring and Control

Introduction

The measuring and control of services is based on a continuous cycle of monitoring, reporting and initiating action. We will discuss this cycle in detail because it is essential to the supply, support and improvement of services.

Basic concepts

Three terms play a leading role in monitoring and control:
* monitoring
* reporting
* control

Monitoring refers to the observation of a situation to discover changes that occur over time.

Reporting refers to the analysis, production and distribution of the output of the activity that is being monitored.

Control refers to the management of the usefulness or behavior of a device, system or service. There are three conditions for control:
the action must ensure that the behavior conforms to a defined standard or norm
the conditions leading to the action must be defined, understood and confirmed
the action must be defined, approved and suitable for these conditions

Activities, methods and techniques

The monitoring/control cycle

The best-known model for the description of control is the monitoring/control cycle. Although it is a simple model it has many complex applications in IT service management. In this section we describe the basic concepts of the model. Next we will show how important these concepts are for the service management lifecycle. Figure 5.5 reflects the basic principles of control.

This cycle measures an activity and its benefits by means of a pre-defined norm or standard to determine whether the results are within the target values for performance or quality. If this is not the case, action must be taken to improve the situation or resume the normal performance.

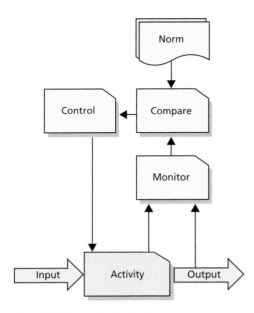

Figure 5.5 The monitoring/control cycle

There are two types of monitoring/control cycles:
- **Open cycle systems** are designed for a specific activity, irrespective of the environmental conditions; making a backup, for instance, can be initiated at a specified moment and be completed regardless of other conditions.
- **Closed cycle systems** - Monitoring of an environment and responding to changes in this environment; if, in a network, the network transactions exceed a certain number, the control system will redirect the "traffic" via a backup circuit in order to regulate the network transactions.

Figure 5.6 shows a **complex monitoring/control cycle**: a process that consists of three important activities. Each activity has an input and output and in turn this output is the input for the next activity. Every activity is controlled by its own monitoring/control cycle with the aid of a series of norms for that specific activity. A coordinating monitoring/control cycle monitors the entire process and ensures that all norms are suitable and are being complied with.

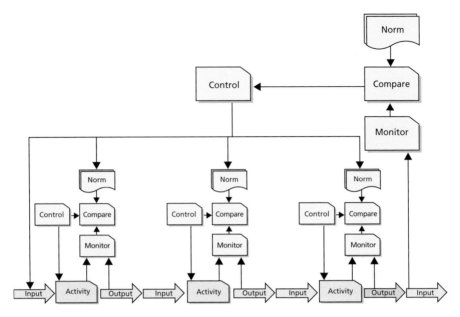

Figure 5.6 The complex monitoring/control cycle

The monitoring/control cycle concept can be used to manage:
- the performance of activities in a process or procedure; in theory every activity and its related output can be measured to ensure that problems in the process are identified before the process is completed
- the effectiveness of the process or procedure as a whole
- the performance of a device or a series of devices

Answer the following questions to determine how the concept of monitoring/control cycles can be used in service management:
- How do we define what we need to monitor?
- How do we monitor (manually or automated)?
- What is a normal process?
- What do we depend on for a normal process?
- What happens before we receive the input?
- How often do we need to measure?

Figure 5.7 shows an **IT service management monitoring/control cycle** and shows how the control of a process or the components of that process can be used to provide a service.

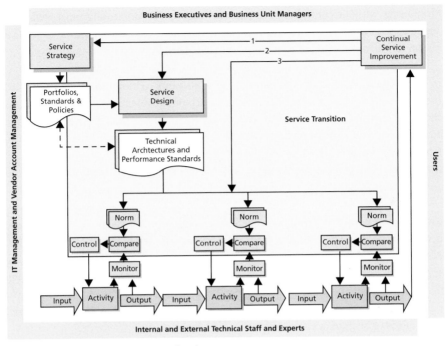

Figure 5.7 The ITSM monitoring/control cycle

There are two levels of monitoring:
- **internal monitoring and control** - focuses on activities and items that take place within a team or department, for instance a service desk manager who monitors the number of calls to determine how many members of staff are needed to answer the telephones
- **external monitoring and control** - the server management team monitors (on behalf of other groups) the CPU performance on important servers and keeps the workload under control; this allows essential applications to perform within the target values set by the application management

This distinction is important. If Service Operation focuses only on internal monitoring the infrastructure is well organized, but the organization has no idea what the quality of the services is or how they can improve this quality. If the organization focuses only on external monitoring it understands how bad the quality of the service is, but it does not know what causes this or how it can change this. In practice, most organizations use a combination of internal and external monitoring, but in many cases they are not linked.

Monitoring without control is irrelevant and ineffective. Monitoring must always be aimed at achieving the service and operational objectives. If, therefore, there is no clear reason for the monitoring of a system or service, there should be no monitoring.

In order for an organization to determine what it wants to monitor, therefore, it must first define the desired outcome: **monitoring and control objectives**. Ideally this process should start with the definition of *Service Level Requirements*. These will specify how the customers and users measure the quality of the service. In addition, these Service Level Requirements provide the input for the Service Design processes.
Availability management, for instance, will determine how the infrastructure must be configured to achieve the fewest possible disruptions.

An important part in determining what Service Operation will be monitoring and how it will get the processes under control is identifying the stakeholders of each service. A stakeholder can be defined as being anyone who has an interest in IT services being successfully supplied and received. Each stakeholder will consider, from his own perspective, what is necessary to provide or receive an IT service. Service Operation must know what these perspectives are in order to determine what needs to be monitored and what needs to be done with the output.

Tools
There are different types of monitoring tools, whereby the situation determines which **type of monitoring** is used:
- **Active versus passive monitoring**:
  - *Active monitoring* refers to the continuous "interrogation" of a device or system in order to determine its status.
  - *Passive monitoring* is more commonly known and refers to generating and passing on events to a device or monitoring agent.
- **Reactive versus proactive monitoring**:
  - *Reactive monitoring* is designed to request an action after a certain type of event or disruption.
  - *Proactive monitoring* is used to trace patterns of events that indicate that a system or device may break down. Proactive monitoring is generally used in more mature environments, where these patterns can be detected earlier.
- **Continuous measuring versus exception-based measuring**:
  - *Continuous measuring* is aimed at the real-time monitoring of a system to ensure that it complies with a certain performance norm. As an example, an application server is available 99% of the agreed access time.

- *Exception-based measuring* does not measure the current performance of a service or system, but discovers and reports exceptions. An example is the generation of an event if a transaction is not completed. It is used for less essential systems or for systems where costs are important.
- **Performance versus output** - There is an important distinction between reporting on the performance of components, teams or a department (*performance*) and reporting that shows that the service quality objectives (*output*) have been achieved. Service Operation carries out both types of monitoring, but ITIL focuses mainly on performance monitoring.

Metrics
It is important that organizations have robust measuring techniques and values that support their objectives. In this context, the following concepts are relevant:
- **Measuring** - Refers to all techniques that evaluate the scope, dimension or capacity of an item in relation to a standard or unit. Measuring is only useful when it is possible to measure the actual output of a system, function or process against a standard or desired level. For instance, a server must be capable of processing a minimum of 100 standard transactions per minute.
- **Metrics** - Concern the quantitative, periodic evaluation of a process, system or function, together with the procedures and tools that are used for this evaluation, and the procedures for interpreting them. This definition is important because it not only specifies what must be measured, but also how the measuring must be done, what the acceptable lower and upper performance limits are and what actions are necessary in the case of normal performance or an exception.
- **Key Performance Indicators (KPIs)** - Refer to a specific, agreed performance level to measure the effectiveness of an organization or process. KPIs are unique to each organization and are related to specific input, output and activities.

5.7 IT Operations

Introduction

To deliver the services as agreed with the customer, the service provider will first have to manage the technical infrastructure that is used to deliver the services. If no new customers are added and no new services have to be introduced, if no incidents occur in existing services, and if no changes have to be made in existing services - even then, the IT organization will be busy with a range of Service Operations. These activities focus on actually delivering the agreed service as agreed.

Operations bridge

The operations bridge is a central point of coordination that manages various events and routine operational activities, and reports on the status or performance of technological components.

An operations bridge brings together all vital observation points in the IT infrastructure so that they can be monitored and managed with minimum effort in a central location.

The operations bridge combines a great many activities, such as console management, event handling, first line network management and support outside office hours. In some organizations, the service desk is a part of the operations bridge.

Activities, methods and techniques

Job scheduling

IT operations executes standard routines, queries or reports that technical and application management teams have handed over as part of the service or of routine daily maintenance tasks.

Backup and restore

Essentially, backup and restore is a component of good continuity planning. Service Design must therefore ensure that there are good backup strategies for every service. Service Transition must ensure that they are tested in the right way.

Furthermore, some organizations - such as financial service providers and listed companies - must implement and monitor a formal backup and restore strategy as required by the law and regulations. The precise requirements vary per country and industry.

An organization must protect its data, which includes **backup** and storage of data in reserved locations where it is protected and, if necessary, accessible.

A complete backup strategy must be agreed with the business, which must cover the following elements:
- what data should the backup include, and how often must it be made?
- how many generations of data must be retained?
- the backup type and the checkpoints that are used
- the locations used for storage and the rotation schedule
- transport methods
- required tests
- planned recovery point; the point to which data must be recovered after an IT service resumes
- planned recovery time; the maximum allowed time to resume an IT service after an interruption
- how will it be checked that the backups are functional when they need to be restored?

In all cases, the IT operations staff must be qualified in backup and restore procedures. These procedures must be documented properly in the procedure manual of IT operations. Where necessary, you should include specific requirements or targets in OLAs or UCs, and specify user or customer obligations and activities in the relevant SLA.

A **restore** can be initiated from several sources, varying from an event indicating data corruption to a *service request* from a user or customer. A restore may be necessary in case of:
- corrupt data
- lost data
- a calamity plan / IT service continuity situation
- historical data required for forensic investigation

Print and output

Many services provide their information in **print** or electronic form (**output**). The service provider must ensure that the information ends up in the right places, correctly and in the right form. Information security often plays a part in this respect.

The customer should notify the service provider in time of a temporarily increased need for print and output.

Laws and regulations may play an important part in print and output. Archiving important or sensitive data is particularly important.

Service providers are generally deemed to be responsible for maintaining the infrastructure to make the print and output available to the customer (printers, storage). In this case, that task must be laid down in the SLA.

5.8 Service Desk

A service desk is a **functional unit** with associates involved in differing service events. These service events come in by phone, internet or infrastructure, events which are reported automatically.

The service desk is a very important element of the IT department of an organization. It must be the only contact point for IT users and it deals with all incidents and service requests. The associates often use software tools to record and manage all events.

Justification and role of a service desk

Many organizations consider a service desk the best means for a first line support in case of IT problems. A service desk offers the following benefits:

- improved customer service, better perception of the service on the part of the client and greater client satisfaction
- greater access through one single contact, communication and information point
- client and user requests are resolved better and quicker
- improved cooperation and communication
- less negative impact on business
- better managed and controlled infrastructure
- better use of resources through IT support and increased productivity of company associates
- more meaningful management information for decisions concerning support

Service desk objectives

The primary purpose of the service desk is to resume "normal service" to the user as soon as possible. This may be resolving a technical error, but also filling a service request or answering a question.

Organizational structure of a service desk

There are many ways to organize a service desk. The solution will be different for each organization. The most important options are:

- local service desk
- centralized service desk
- virtual service desk
- 24-hour service
- specialized service desk groups

These options are elaborated further below. In practice, an organization will implement a structure that combines a number of these options in order to satisfy the needs of the business.

The **local service desk** is located at or physically close to the users it is supporting. Because of this, communications are often much smoother and the visible presence is attractive for some users. However, a local service desk is expensive and may be inefficient if the amount of service events does not really justify a service desk.

There may be a few sound reasons for maintaining a local service desk:
- linguistic, cultural and political differences
- different time zones
- specialized groups of users
- existence of adjusted or special services for which specialized knowledge is required
- status of the users

The number of service desks can be reduced by installing them at one single location (or by reducing the number of local service desks). In that case, the associates are assigned to one or more **centralized service desk** structures. This may be less expensive and more efficient, because fewer associates can deal with the service events (calls), while the level of knowledge of the service desk is bound to increase.

By using technology, specifically the internet, and the use of support tools, it is possible to create the impression of a centralized service desk, whereas the associates are in fact spread out over a number of geographic or structural locations: this is the **virtual service desk**.

Some international organizations like to combine two or more geographically spread out service desks in order to offer a **24/7 service**. In this way, a service desk in Asia, for example, can deal with incoming service events during standard office hours, whereby at the end of that period, a service desk in Europe takes care of any outstanding events. That desk deals with those service events together with its own events and at the end of the day, responsibility is transferred to a service desk in America, which then returns responsibility to the Asian service desk, thus completing the cycle.

It may be attractive for some organizations to create specialized **service desk groups**, so that incidents relating to a specific IT service are routed straight to the specialized group. In this way, incidents can be resolved more promptly.

The **environment** of the service desk must be carefully selected, preferably a location where workstations have adequate space with natural light. A quiet environment with good acoustics is equally important, because the associates should not be bothered by each other's telephone conversations. Ergonomic office furniture is also important.

Service desk personnel

Care should be taken that a sufficient **number of associates** are available, so that the service desk can meet the business demand at any time. The number of service events can, of course, strongly fluctuate from day-to-day and hour to hour. An organization will take peak hours and quiet periods into account.

A decision should be made as to which skill levels are necessary for the service desk personnel. To determine the required **skill level**, weigh the arranged resolution times against the complexity of the **supported systems**, and "the outlay the business is willing to pay". The optimal and most efficient approach is generally a first line support via the service desk, which records the service event and transmits escalations promptly to more expert second-level and third-level support groups.

If the skill levels have been established, the service desk must be directed in a way that the associates receive and maintain the necessary skills. During all work hours, there has to be a good mix of skills present.

It is essential that all service desk associates receive sufficient **training**. All new associates must follow a formal introduction program. The precise content of it will vary with each new associate, subject to the existing expertise and experience.

In order to keep the service desk associates up-to-date, a program is necessary so that they can be kept informed of new developments, services and techniques. The timing of these type of activities is essential, because they should not impact the normal tasks. Many service desks organize short training sessions during quiet periods when the associates are handling fewer service events.

It is very important that all IT associates realize the importance of the service desk and the people working there. A considerable attrition of associates has a disturbing effect and can lead to an incoherent service. Thus the managers have to engage in efforts **to retain the associates**.

Many organizations find it meaningful to appoint a number of so-called **super users** in the user community. They function as contact persons with the IT organization in general and the service desk in particular.

Organizations can provide the super users extra training and use them as communication channel. They can be asked to filter requests and certain problems on behalf of the user community. If an important service or component is down, causing an extra burden for many users, this may lead to many reactions coming in.

Super users do not provide support for the entire IT. In many cases, the super user will offer support only for a specific application, module or business unit. As a business user a super user often has thorough knowledge of important company processes and knows how services are working in practice. It is very useful to share this with the service desk, so that it can offer better quality services in the future.

Metrics

In order to evaluate the performance of the service desk at regular time intervals, **metrics** must be established. In this way, the maturity, efficiency, effectiveness and potentials can be established and the service desk actions improved.

Metrics for the performance of a service desk must be selected carefully and realistically. It is common to select those metrics which are readily available and which point to a possible indicator for the performance. However, this can be misleading. The total number of service events that a service desk has received, for example, is not an indicator by itself of a good or bad performance, and can, in fact, be caused by events which do not impact on the service desk.

In order to determine this, further analysis and more detailed metrics are necessary which are researched for a certain period of time. Besides the statistics mentioned earlier regarding the handling of service events, the metrics consist, among others, of:

- first line handling time; the percentage of service events, which are resolved by the first level, without the necessity to escalate to other support groups
- average time to resolve an incident (or other type of service call) (if it is resolved by the first level)
- average time to escalate an incident (if a first line solution is not possible)
- average handling costs of an incident

- percentage of client and user updates which are executed within the target values, as set forth in the SLA objectives
- average time to evaluate and close out a resolved incident

Besides following "hard" metrics in the performance of the service desk, it is also important to carry out "soft" metrics: **the client and user Satisfaction Surveys** (e.g. Do clients and users find that their phone calls are properly answered? Was the service desk associate friendly and professional?). User or client can best complete this type of metrics, but specific questions about the service desk itself may also be asked.

Outsourcing the service desk

The decision to contract out or outsource is a strategic subject for Senior Managers. Regardless of the reasons for outsourcing or the size of the outsource contract, it is important that the organization remains responsible for the activities and services rendered by the service desk. The organization is ultimately responsible for the outcome of the decision and must therefore decide which service is going to be offered.

If the service desk is being outsourced, the **tools** must be consistent with the tools being used by the organizations client. Outsourcing is frequently seen as a chance to replace obsolescent or inadequate tools; however, serious integration problems often arise between the new and existing tools and processes.

Ideally, the service desk being outsourced must use the same **tools and processes** to enable a smooth process stream between the service desk and the second and third level support groups.

The **SLA targets** for incident handling and handling times must be arranged with the clients and between all teams and departments; OLA and underlying contract objectives must be coordinated and in tune with separate support groups, so that they support the SLA targets.

Acronyms

AMIS	Availability Management Information System
APMG	APM Group
BCM	Business Continuity Management
BCP	Business Continuity Plan
BCS	British Computer Society
BIA	Business Impact Analysis
BPO	Business Process Outsourcing
BU	Business Unit
CAB	Change Advisory Board
CCM	Component Capacity Management
CFIA	Component Failure Impact Analysis
CI	Configuration Item
CMDB	Configuration Management Database
CMIS	Capacity Management Information System
CMS	Configuration Management System
CS	Change Schedule
CSF	Critical Success Factor
CSI	Continual Service Improvement
CSP	Core Service Package
DIKW	Data Information Knowledge Wisdom
DML	Definitive Media Library
ECAB	Emergency Change Advisory Board
ELS	Early Life Support
FTA	Fault Tree Analysis
HR	Human Resources

ISMS	Information Security Management System
ITIL	Information Technology Infrastructure Library
ITSCM	IT Service Continuity Management
itSMF	IT Service Management Forum
KEDB	Known Error Database
KPI	Key Performance Indicator
KPO	Knowledge Process Outsourcing
LCS	Loyalist Certification Services
LOS	Line of Service
M_o_R	Management of Risk
MTBF	Mean Time Between Failures
MTBSI	Mean Time Between Service Incidents
MTTR	Mean Time To Repair
MTRS	Mean Time to Restore Service
OGC	Office of Government Commerce
OLA	Operational Level Agreement
PBA	Pattern of Business Activity
PDCA	Plan Do Check Act
PFS	Prerequisites for Success
PIR	Post-Implementation Review
PRINCE2	PRojects IN Controlled Environments
PSA	Projected Service Availability
PSO	Projected Service Outage
RAD	Rapid Application Development
RFC	Request for Change
SAC	Service Acceptance Criteria
SACM	Service Asset and Configuration Management
SCD	Supplier and Contract Database
SCM	Service Catalogue Management
SDP	Service Design Package
SFA	Service Failure Analysis
SIP	Service Improvement Plan
SKMS	Service Knowledge Management System
SLA	Service Level Agreement
SLM	Service Level Management
SLP	Service Level Package
SLR	Service Level Requirement
SOC	Separation of Concerns
SPM	Service Portfolio Management

SPOC	Single Point of Contact
SPOF	Single Point of Failure
TCU	Total Cost of Utilization
TSO	The Stationary Office
UC	Underpinning Contract
VBF	Vital Business Function
VCD	Variable Cost Dynamics

Glossary

Where a term is relevant to a particular phase in the Lifecycle of an IT Service, or to one of the Core ITIL publications, this is indicated at the beginning of the definition. This glossary is based on the official ITIL V3 Glossary, version 01 of 30 May 2007.

Acceptance
: Formal agreement that an IT Service, Process, Plan, or other Deliverable is complete, accurate, Reliable and meets its specified Requirements. Acceptance is usually preceded by Evaluation or Testing and is often required before proceeding to the next stage of a Project or Process.
See Service Acceptance Criteria.

Access Management
: (Service Operation) The Process responsible for allowing Users to make use of IT Services, data, or other Assets. Access Management helps to protect the Confidentiality, Integrity and Availability of Assets by ensuring that only authorized Users are able to access or modify the Assets. Access Management is sometimes referred to as Rights Management or Identity Management.

Account Manager
: (Service Strategy) A Role that is very similar to Business Relationship Manager, but includes more commercial aspects. Most commonly used when dealing with External Customers.

Accounting
: (Service Strategy) The Process responsible for identifying actual Costs of delivering IT Services, comparing these with budgeted costs, and managing variance from the Budget.

Accredited
: Officially authorized to carry out a Role. For example an Accredited body may be authorized to provide training or to conduct Audits.

Active Monitoring
: (Service Operation) Monitoring of a Configuration Item or an IT Service that uses automated regular checks to discover the current status.
See Passive Monitoring.

Activity	A set of actions designed to achieve a particular result. Activities are usually defined as part of Processes or Plans, and are documented in Procedures.
Agreed Service Time	(Service Design) A synonym for Service Hours, commonly used in formal calculations of Availability. See Downtime.
Agreement	A Document that describes a formal understanding between two or more parties. An Agreement is not legally binding, unless it forms part of a Contract. See Service Level Agreement, Operational Level Agreement.
Alert	(Service Operation) A warning that a threshold has been reached, something has changed, or a Failure has occurred. Alerts are often created and managed by System Management tools and are managed by the Event Management Process.
Analytical Modeling	(Service Strategy) (Service Design) (Continual Service Improvement) A technique that uses mathematical Models to predict the behavior of a Configuration Item or IT Service. Analytical Models are commonly used in Capacity Management and Availability Management. See Modeling.
Application	Software that provides Functions that are required by an IT Service. Each Application may be part of more than one IT Service. An Application runs on one or more Servers or Clients. See Application Management, Application Portfolio.
Application Management	(Service Design) (Service Operation) The Function responsible for managing Applications throughout their Lifecycle.
Application Portfolio	(Service Design) A database or structured Document used to manage Applications throughout their Lifecycle. The Application Portfolio contains key Attributes of all Applications. The Application Portfolio is sometimes implemented as part of the Service Portfolio, or as part of the Configuration Management System.
Application Service Provider (ASP)	(Service Design) An External Service Provider that provides IT Services using Applications running at the Service Provider's premises. Users access the Applications by network connections to the Service Provider.
Application Sizing	(Service Design) The Activity responsible for understanding the Resource Requirements needed to support a new Application, or a major Change to an existing Application. Application Sizing helps to ensure that the IT Service can meet its agreed Service Level Targets for Capacity and Performance.
Architecture	(Service Design) The structure of a System or IT Service, including the Relationships of Components to each other and to the environment they are in. Architecture also includes the Standards and Guidelines which guide the design and evolution of the System.
Assembly	(Service Transition) A Configuration Item that is made up from a number of other CIs. For example a Server CI may contain CIs for CPUs, Disks, Memory etc.; an IT Service CI may contain many Hardware, Software and other CIs. See Component CI, Build.

Assessment	Inspection and analysis to check whether a Standard or set of Guidelines is being followed, that Records are accurate, or that Efficiency and Effectiveness targets are being met. See Audit.
Asset	(Service Strategy) Any Resource or Capability. Assets of a Service Provider include anything that could contribute to the delivery of a Service. Assets can be one of the following types: Management, Organization, Process, Knowledge, People, Information, Applications, Infrastructure, and Financial Capital.
Asset Management	(Service Transition) Asset Management is the Process responsible for tracking and reporting the value and ownership of financial Assets throughout their Lifecycle. Asset Management is part of an overall Service Asset and Configuration Management Process. See Asset Register.
Asset Register	(Service Transition) A list of Assets, which includes their ownership and value. The Asset Register is maintained by Asset Management.
Attribute	(Service Transition) A piece of information about a Configuration Item. Examples are name, location, Version number, and Cost. Attributes of CIs are recorded in the Configuration Management Database (CMDB). See Relationship.
Audit	Formal inspection and verification to check whether a Standard or set of Guidelines is being followed, that Records are accurate, or that Efficiency and Effectiveness targets are being met. An Audit may be carried out by internal or external groups. See Certification, Assessment.
Authority Matrix	Synonym for RACI.
Automatic Call Distribution (ACD)	(Service Operation) Use of Information Technology to direct an incoming telephone call to the most appropriate person in the shortest possible time. ACD is sometimes called Automated Call Distribution.
Availability	(Service Design) Ability of a Configuration Item or IT Service to perform its agreed Function when required. Availability is determined by Reliability, Maintainability, Serviceability, Performance, and Security. Availability is usually calculated as a percentage. This calculation is often based on Agreed Service Time and Downtime. It is Best Practice to calculate Availability using measurements of the Business output of the IT Service.
Availability Management	(Service Design) The Process responsible for defining, analyzing, Planning, measuring and improving all aspects of the Availability of IT Services. Availability Management is responsible for ensuring that all IT Infrastructure, Processes, Tools, Roles etc are appropriate for the agreed Service Level Targets for Availability.

Availability Management Information System (AMIS)	(Service Design) A virtual repository of all Availability Management data, usually stored in multiple physical locations. See Service Knowledge Management System.
Availability Plan	(Service Design) A Plan to ensure that existing and future Availability Requirements for IT Services can be provided Cost Effectively.
Back-out	Synonym for Remediation.
Backup	(Service Design) (Service Operation) Copying data to protect against loss of Integrity or Availability of the original.
Balanced Scorecard	(Continual Service Improvement) A management tool developed by Drs. Robert Kaplan (Harvard Business School) and David Norton. A Balanced Scorecard enables a Strategy to be broken down into Key Performance Indicators. Performance against the KPIs is used to demonstrate how well the Strategy is being achieved. A Balanced Scorecard has 4 major areas, each of which has a small number of KPIs. The same 4 areas are considered at different levels of detail throughout the Organization.
Baseline	(Continual Service Improvement) A Benchmark used as a reference point. For example: • An ITSM Baseline can be used as a starting point to measure the effect of a Service Improvement Plan • A Performance Baseline can be used to measure changes in Performance over the lifetime of an IT Service • A Configuration Management Baseline can be used to enable the IT Infrastructure to be restored to a known Configuration if a Change or Release fails
Benchmark	(Continual Service Improvement) The recorded state of something at a specific point in time. A Benchmark can be created for a Configuration, a Process, or any other set of data. For example, a benchmark can be used in: • Continual Service Improvement, to establish the current state for managing improvements. • Capacity Management, to document Performance characteristics during normal operations. • See Benchmarking, Baseline.
Benchmarking	(Continual Service Improvement) Comparing a Benchmark with a Baseline or with Best Practice. The term Benchmarking is also used to mean creating a series of Benchmarks over time, and comparing the results to measure progress or improvement.
Best Practice	Proven Activities or Processes that have been successfully used by multiple Organizations. ITIL is an example of Best Practice.

Brainstorming	(Service Design) A technique that helps a team to generate ideas. Ideas are not reviewed during the Brainstorming session, but at a later stage. Brainstorming is often used by Problem Management to identify possible causes.
British Standards Institution (BSI)	The UK National Standards body, responsible for creating and maintaining British Standards. See http://www.bsi-global.com for more information. See ISO.
Budget	A list of all the money an Organization or Business Unit plans to receive, and plans to pay out, over a specified period of time. See Budgeting, Planning.
Budgeting	The Activity of predicting and controlling the spending of money. Consists of a periodic negotiation cycle to set future Budgets (usually annual) and the day-to-day monitoring and adjusting of current Budgets.
Build	(Service Transition) The Activity of assembling a number of Configuration Items to create part of an IT Service. The term Build is also used to refer to a Release that is authorized for distribution. For example Server Build or laptop Build. See Configuration Baseline.
Build Environment	(Service Transition) A controlled Environment where Applications, IT Services and other Builds are assembled prior to being moved into a Test or Live Environment.
Business	(Service Strategy) An overall corporate entity or Organization formed of a number of Business Units. In the context of ITSM, the term Business includes public sector and not-for-profit organizations, as well as companies. An IT Service Provider provides IT Services to a Customer within a Business. The IT Service Provider may be part of the same Business as their Customer (Internal Service Provider), or part of another Business (External Service Provider).
Business Capacity Management (BCM)	(Service Design) In the context of ITSM, Business Capacity Management is the Activity responsible for understanding future Business Requirements for use in the Capacity Plan. See Service Capacity Management.
Business Case	(Service Strategy) Justification for a significant item of expenditure. Includes information about Costs, benefits, options, issues, Risks, and possible problems. See Cost Benefit Analysis.
Business Continuity Management (BCM)	(Service Design) The Business Process responsible for managing Risks that could seriously impact the Business. BCM safeguards the interests of key stakeholders, reputation, brand and value creating activities. The BCM Process involves reducing Risks to an acceptable level and planning for the recovery of Business Processes should a disruption to the Business occur. BCM sets the Objectives, Scope and Requirements for IT Service Continuity Management.

Business Continuity Plan (BCP) (Service Design) A Plan defining the steps required to Restore Business Processes following a disruption. The Plan will also identify the triggers for Invocation, people to be involved, communications etc. IT Service Continuity Plans form a significant part of Business Continuity Plans.

Business Customer (Service Strategy) A recipient of a product or a Service from the Business. For example if the Business is a car manufacturer then the Business Customer is someone who buys a car.

Business Impact Analysis (BIA) (Service Strategy) BIA is the Activity in Business Continuity Management that identifies Vital Business Functions and their dependencies. These dependencies may include Suppliers, people, other Business Processes, IT Services etc.
BIA defines the recovery requirements for IT Services. These requirements include Recovery Time Objectives, Recovery Point Objectives and minimum Service Level Targets for each IT Service.

Business Objective (Service Strategy) The Objective of a Business Process, or of the Business as a whole. Business Objectives support the Business Vision, provide guidance for the IT Strategy, and are often supported by IT Services.

Business Operations (Service Strategy) The day-to-day execution, monitoring and management of Business Processes.

Business Perspective (Continual Service Improvement) An understanding of the Service Provider and IT Services from the point of view of the Business, and an understanding of the Business from the point of view of the Service Provider.

Business Process A Process that is owned and carried out by the Business. A Business Process contributes to the delivery of a product or Service to a Business Customer. For example, a retailer may have a purchasing Process which helps to deliver Services to their Business Customers. Many Business Processes rely on IT Services.

Business Relationship Management (Service Strategy) The Process or Function responsible for maintaining a Relationship with the Business. BRM usually includes:
- Managing personal Relationships with Business managers
- Providing input to Service Portfolio Management
- Ensuring that the IT Service Provider is satisfying the Business needs of the Customers

This Process has strong links with Service Level Management.

Business Relationship Manager (BRM) (Service Strategy) A Role responsible for maintaining the Relationship with one or more Customers. This Role is often combined with the Service Level Manager Role.
See Account Manager.

Business Service
An IT Service that directly supports a Business Process, as opposed to an Infrastructure Service which is used internally by the IT Service Provider and is not usually visible to the Business.
The term Business Service is also used to mean a Service that is delivered to Business Customers by Business Units. For example delivery of financial services to Customers of a bank, or goods to the Customers of a retail store. Successful delivery of Business Services often depends on one or more IT Services.

Business Service Management (BSM)
(Service Strategy) (Service Design) An approach to the management of IT Services that considers the Business Processes supported and the Business value provided. This term also means the management of Business Services delivered to Business Customers.

Business Unit
(Service Strategy) A segment of the Business which has its own Plans, Metrics, income and Costs. Each Business Unit owns Assets and uses these to create value for Customers in the form of goods and Services.

Call
(Service Operation) A telephone call to the Service Desk from a User. A Call could result in an Incident or a Service Request being logged.

Call Centre
(Service Operation) An Organization or Business Unit which handles large numbers of incoming and outgoing telephone calls.
See Service Desk.

Call Type
(Service Operation) A Category that is used to distinguish incoming requests to a Service Desk. Common Call Types are Incident, Service Request and Complaint.

Capability
(Service Strategy) The ability of an Organization, person, Process, Application, Configuration Item or IT Service to carry out an Activity. Capabilities are intangible Assets of an Organization.
See Resource.

Capability Maturity Model (CMM)
(Continual Service Improvement) The Capability Maturity Model for Software (also known as the CMM and SW-CMM) is a model used to identify Best Practices to help increase Process Maturity. CMM was developed at the Software Engineering Institute (SEI) of Carnegie Mellon University. In 2000, the SW-CMM was upgraded to CMMI® (Capability Maturity Model Integration). The SEI no longer maintains the SW-CMM model, its associated appraisal methods, or training materials.

Capability Maturity Model Integration (CMMI)
(Continual Service Improvement) Capability Maturity Model® Integration (CMMI) is a process improvement approach developed by the Software Engineering Institute (SEI) of Carnegie Melon University. CMMI provides organizations with the essential elements of effective processes. It can be used to guide process improvement across a project, a division, or an entire organization. CMMI helps integrate traditionally separate organizational functions, set process improvement goals and priorities, provide guidance for quality processes, and provide a point of reference for appraising current processes. See http://www.sei.cmu.edu/cmmi/ for more information.
See CMM, Continuous Improvement, Maturity.

Capacity	(Service Design) The maximum Throughput that a Configuration Item or IT Service can deliver whilst meeting agreed Service Level Targets. For some types of CI, Capacity may be the size or volume, for example a disk drive.
Capacity Management	(Service Design) The Process responsible for ensuring that the Capacity of IT Services and the IT Infrastructure is able to deliver agreed Service Level Targets in a Cost Effective and timely manner. Capacity Management considers all Resources required to deliver the IT Service, and plans for short, medium and long term Business Requirements.
Capacity Management Information System (CMIS)	(Service Design) A virtual repository of all Capacity Management data, usually stored in multiple physical locations. See Service Knowledge Management System.
Capacity Plan	(Service Design) A Capacity Plan is used to manage the Resources required to deliver IT Services. The Plan contains scenarios for different predictions of Business demand, and costed options to deliver the agreed Service Level Targets.
Capacity Planning	(Service Design) The Activity within Capacity Management responsible for creating a Capacity Plan.
Capital Expenditure (CAPEX)	(Service Strategy) The Cost of purchasing something that will become a financial Asset, for example computer equipment and buildings. The value of the Asset is Depreciated over multiple accounting periods.
Capital Item	(Service Strategy) An Asset that is of interest to Financial Management because it is above an agreed financial value.
Capitalization	(Service Strategy) Identifying major Cost as capital, even though no Asset is purchased. This is done to spread the impact of the Cost over multiple accounting periods. The most common example of this is software development, or purchase of a software license.
Category	A named group of things that have something in common. Categories are used to group similar things together. For example Cost Types are used to group similar types of Cost. Incident Categories are used to group similar types of Incident, CI Types are used to group similar types of Configuration Item.
Certification	Issuing a certificate to confirm Compliance to a Standard. Certification includes a formal Audit by an independent and Accredited body. The term Certification is also used to mean awarding a certificate to verify that a person has achieved a qualification.
Change	(Service Transition) The addition, modification or removal of anything that could have an effect on IT Services. The Scope should include all IT Services, Configuration Items, Processes, Documentation etc.
Change Advisory Board (CAB)	(Service Transition) A group of people that advises the Change Manager in the Assessment, prioritization and scheduling of Changes. This board is usually made up of representatives from all areas within the IT Service Provider, the Business, and Third Parties such as Suppliers.

Change Case   (Service Operation) A technique used to predict the impact of proposed Changes. Change Cases use specific scenarios to clarify the scope of proposed Changes and to help with Cost Benefit Analysis.
See Use Case.

Change History   (Service Transition) Information about all changes made to a Configuration Item during its life. Change History consists of all those Change Records that apply to the CI.

Change Management   (Service Transition) The Process responsible for controlling the Lifecycle of all Changes. The primary objective of Change Management is to enable beneficial Changes to be made, with minimum disruption to IT Services.

Change Model   (Service Transition) A repeatable way of dealing with a particular Category of Change. A Change Model defines specific pre-defined steps that will be followed for a Change of this Category. Change Models may be very simple, with no requirement for approval (e.g. Password Reset) or may be very complex with many steps that require approval (e.g. major software Release).
See Standard Change, Change Advisory Board.

Change Record   (Service Transition) A Record containing the details of a Change. Each Change Record documents the Lifecycle of a single Change. A Change Record is created for every Request for Change that is received, even those that are subsequently rejected. Change Records should reference the Configuration Items that are affected by the Change. Change Records are stored in the Configuration Management System.

Change Request   Synonym for Request for Change.

Change Schedule   (Service Transition) A Document that lists all approved Changes and their planned implementation dates. A Change Schedule is sometimes called a Forward Schedule of Change, even though it also contains information about Changes that have already been implemented.

Change Window   (Service Transition) A regular, agreed time when Changes or Releases may be implemented with minimal impact on Services. Change Windows are usually documented in SLAs.

Charging   (Service Strategy) Requiring payment for IT Services. Charging for IT Services is optional, and many Organizations choose to treat their IT Service Provider as a Cost Centre.

Chronological Analysis   (Service Operation) A technique used to help identify possible causes of Problems. All available data about the Problem is collected and sorted by date and time to provide a detailed timeline. This can make it possible to identify which Events may have been triggered by others.

CI Type   (Service Transition) A Category that is used to Classify CIs. The CI Type identifies the required Attributes and Relationships for a Configuration Record. Common CI Types include: hardware, Document, User etc.

Classification	The act of assigning a Category to something. Classification is used to ensure consistent management and reporting. CIs, Incidents, Problems, Changes etc. are usually classified.
Client	A generic term that means a Customer, the Business or a Business Customer. For example Client Manager may be used as a synonym for Account Manager. The term client is also used to mean: • A computer that is used directly by a User, for example a PC, Handheld Computer, or Workstation. • The part of a Client-Server Application that the User directly interfaces with. For example an email Client.
Closed	(Service Operation) The final Status in the Lifecycle of an Incident, Problem, Change etc. When the Status is Closed, no further action is taken.
Closure	(Service Operation) The act of changing the Status of an Incident, Problem, Change etc. to Closed.
COBIT	(Continual Service Improvement) Control Objectives for Information and related Technology (COBIT) provides guidance and Best Practice for the management of IT Processes. COBIT is published by the IT Governance Institute. See http://www.isaca.org/ for more information.
Code of Practice	A Guideline published by a public body or a Standards Organization, such as ISO or BSI. Many Standards consist of a Code of Practice and a Specification. The Code of Practice describes recommended Best Practice.
Cold Standby	Synonym for Gradual Recovery.
Commercial off the Shelf (COTS)	(Service Design) Application software or Middleware that can be purchased from a Third Party.
Compliance	Ensuring that a Standard or set of Guidelines is followed, or that proper, consistent accounting or other practices are being employed.
Component	A general term that is used to mean one part of something more complex. For example, a computer System may be a component of an IT Service, an Application may be a Component of a Release Unit. Components that need to be managed should be Configuration Items.
Component Capacity Management (CCM)	(Service Design) (Continual Service Improvement) The Process responsible for understanding the Capacity, Utilization, and Performance of Configuration Items. Data is collected, recorded and analyzed for use in the Capacity Plan. See Service Capacity Management.
Component CI	(Service Transition) A Configuration Item that is part of an Assembly. For example, a CPU or Memory CI may be part of a Server CI.
Component Failure Impact Analysis (CFIA)	(Service Design) A technique that helps to identify the impact of CI failure on IT Services. A matrix is created with IT Services on one edge and CIs on the other. This enables the identification of critical CIs (that could cause the failure of multiple IT Services) and of fragile IT Services (that have multiple Single Points of Failure).

Computer Telephony Integration (CTI)	(Service Operation) CTI is a general term covering any kind of integration between computers and telephone Systems. It is most commonly used to refer to Systems where an Application displays detailed screens relating to incoming or outgoing telephone calls. See Automatic Call Distribution, Interactive Voice Response.
Concurrency	A measure of the number of Users engaged in the same Operation at the same time.
Confidentiality	(Service Design) A security principle that requires that data should only be accessed by authorized people.
Configuration	(Service Transition) A generic term, used to describe a group of Configuration Items that work together to deliver an IT Service, or a recognizable part of an IT Service. Configuration is also used to describe the parameter settings for one or more CIs.
Configuration Baseline	(Service Transition) A Baseline of a Configuration that has been formally agreed and is managed through the Change Management process. A Configuration Baseline is used as a basis for future Builds, Releases and Changes.
Configuration Control	(Service Transition) The Activity responsible for ensuring that adding, modifying or removing a CI is properly managed, for example by submitting a Request for Change or Service Request.
Configuration Identification	(Service Transition) The Activity responsible for collecting information about Configuration Items and their Relationships, and loading this information into the CMDB. Configuration Identification is also responsible for labeling the CIs themselves, so that the corresponding Configuration Records can be found.
Configuration Item (CI)	(Service Transition) Any Component that needs to be managed in order to deliver an IT Service. Information about each CI is recorded in a Configuration Record within the Configuration Management System and is maintained throughout its Lifecycle by Configuration Management. CIs are under the control of Change Management. CIs typically include IT Services, hardware, software, buildings, people, and formal documentation such as Process documentation and SLAs.
Configuration Management	(Service Transition) The Process responsible for maintaining information about Configuration Items required to deliver an IT Service, including their Relationships. This information is managed throughout the Lifecycle of the CI. Configuration Management is part of an overall Service Asset and Configuration Management Process.
Configuration Management Database (CMDB)	(Service Transition) A database used to store Configuration Records throughout their Lifecycle. The Configuration Management System maintains one or more CMDBs, and each CMDB stores Attributes of CIs, and Relationships with other CIs.

Configuration Management System (CMS)	(Service Transition) A set of tools and databases that are used to manage an IT Service Provider's Configuration data. The CMS also includes information about Incidents, Problems, Known Errors, Changes and Releases; and may contain data about employees, Suppliers, locations, Business Units, Customers and Users. The CMS includes tools for collecting, storing, managing, updating, and presenting data about all Configuration Items and their Relationships. The CMS is maintained by Configuration Management and is used by all IT Service Management Processes. See Configuration Management Database, Service Knowledge Management System.
Configuration Record	(Service Transition) A Record containing the details of a Configuration Item. Each Configuration Record documents the Lifecycle of a single CI. Configuration Records are stored in a Configuration Management Database.
Configuration Structure	(Service Transition) The hierarchy and other Relationships between all the Configuration Items that comprise a Configuration.
Continual Service Improvement (CSI)	(Continual Service Improvement) A stage in the Lifecycle of an IT Service and the title of one of the Core ITIL publications. Continual Service Improvement is responsible for managing improvements to IT Service Management Processes and IT Services. The Performance of the IT Service Provider is continually measured and improvements are made to Processes, IT Services and IT Infrastructure in order to increase Efficiency, Effectiveness, and Cost Effectiveness. See Plan-Do-Check-Act.
Continuous Availability	(Service Design) An approach or design to achieve 100% Availability. A Continuously Available IT Service has no planned or unplanned Downtime.
Continuous Operation	(Service Design) An approach or design to eliminate planned Downtime of an IT Service. Note that individual Configuration Items may be down even though the IT Service is Available.
Contract	A legally binding Agreement between two or more parties.
Contract Portfolio	(Service Strategy) A database or structured Document used to manage Service Contracts or Agreements between an IT Service Provider and their Customers. Each IT Service delivered to a Customer should have a Contract or other Agreement which is listed in the Contract Portfolio. See Service Portfolio, Service Catalogue.
Control	A means of managing a Risk, ensuring that a Business Objective is achieved, or ensuring that a Process is followed. Example Controls include Policies, Procedures, Roles, RAID, door-locks etc. A control is sometimes called a Countermeasure or safeguard. Control also means to manage the utilization or behavior of a Configuration Item, System or IT Service.

Control Objectives for Information and related Technology (COBIT)	See COBIT.
Control perspective	(Service Strategy) An approach to the management of IT Services, Processes, Functions, Assets etc. There can be several different Control Perspectives on the same IT Service, Process etc., allowing different individuals or teams to focus on what is important and relevant to their specific Role. Example Control Perspectives include Reactive and Proactive management within IT Operations, or a Lifecycle view for an Application Project team.
Control Processes	The ISO/IEC 20000 Process group that includes Change Management and Configuration Management.
Core Service	(Service Strategy) An IT Service that delivers basic Outcomes desired by one or more Customers. See Supporting Service, Core Service Package.
Core Service Package (CSP)	(Service Strategy) A detailed description of a Core Service that may be shared by two or more Service Level Packages. See Service Package.
Cost	The amount of money spent on a specific Activity, IT Service, or Business Unit. Costs consist of real cost (money), notional cost such as people's time, and Depreciation.
Cost Benefit Analysis	An Activity that analyses and compares the Costs and the benefits involved in one or more alternative courses of action. See Business Case, Net Present Value, Internal Rate of Return, Return on Investment, Value on Investment.
Cost Centre	(Service Strategy) A Business Unit or Project to which Costs are assigned. A Cost Centre does not charge for Services provided. An IT Service Provider can be run as a Cost Centre or a Profit Centre.
Cost Effectiveness	A measure of the balance between the Effectiveness and Cost of a Service, Process or activity, A Cost Effective Process is one which achieves its Objectives at minimum Cost. See KPI, Return on Investment, Value for Money.
Cost Element	(Service Strategy) The middle level of category to which Costs are assigned in Budgeting and Accounting. The highest level category is Cost Type. For example a Cost Type of "people" could have cost elements of payroll, staff benefits, expenses, training, overtime etc. Cost Elements can be further broken down to give Cost Units. For example the Cost Element "expenses" could include Cost Units of Hotels, Transport, Meals etc.
Cost Management	(Service Strategy) A general term that is used to refer to Budgeting and Accounting, sometimes used as a synonym for Financial Management

Cost Type

(Service Strategy) The highest level of category to which Costs are assigned in Budgeting and Accounting. For example hardware, software, people, accommodation, external and Transfer.
See Cost Element, Cost Type.

Cost Unit

(Service Strategy) The lowest level of category to which Costs are assigned, Cost Units are usually things that can be easily counted (e.g. staff numbers, software licenses) or things easily measured (e.g. CPU usage, Electricity consumed). Cost Units are included within Cost Elements. For example a Cost Element of "expenses" could include Cost Units of Hotels, Transport, Meals etc.
See Cost Type.

Countermeasure

Can be used to refer to any type of Control. The term Countermeasure is most often used when referring to measures that increase Resilience, Fault Tolerance or Reliability of an IT Service.

Course Corrections

Changes made to a Plan or Activity that has already started, to ensure that it will meet its Objectives. Course corrections are made as a result of Monitoring progress.

CRAMM

A methodology and tool for analyzing and managing Risks. CRAMM was developed by the UK Government, but is now privately owned. Further information is available from http://www.cramm.com/

Crisis Management

The Process responsible for managing the wider implications of Business Continuity. A Crisis Management team is responsible for Strategic issues such as managing media relations and shareholder confidence, and decides when to invoke Business Continuity Plans.

Critical Success Factor (CSF)

Something that must happen if a Process, Project, Plan, or IT Service is to succeed. KPIs are used to measure the achievement of each CSF. For example a CSF of "protect IT Services when making Changes" could be measured by KPIs such as "percentage reduction of unsuccessful Changes", "percentage reduction in Changes causing Incidents" etc.

Culture

A set of values that is shared by a group of people, including expectations about how people should behave, ideas, beliefs, and practices.
See Vision.

Customer

Someone who buys goods or Services. The Customer of an IT Service Provider is the person or group who defines and agrees the Service Level Targets. The term Customers is also sometimes informally used to mean Users, for example "this is a Customer focused Organization".

Customer Portfolio

(Service Strategy) A database or structured Document used to record all Customers of the IT Service Provider. The Customer Portfolio is the Business Relationship Manager's view of the Customers who receive Services from the IT Service Provider.
See Contract Portfolio, Service Portfolio.

Dashboard	(Service Operation) A graphical representation of overall IT Service Performance and Availability. Dashboard images may be updated in real-time, and can also be included in management reports and web pages. Dashboards can be used to support Service Level Management, Event Management or Incident Diagnosis.
Data-to-Information-to-Knowledge-to-Wisdom (DIKW)	A way of understanding the relationships between data, information, knowledge, and wisdom. DIKW shows how each of these builds on the others.
Definitive Media Library (DML)	(Service Transition) One or more locations in which the definitive and approved versions of all software Configuration Items are securely stored. The DML may also contain associated CIs such as licenses and documentation. The DML is a single logical storage area even if there are multiple locations. All software in the DML is under the control of Change and Release Management and is recorded in the Configuration Management System. Only software from the DML is acceptable for use in a Release.
Deliverable	Something that must be provided to meet a commitment in a Service Level Agreement or a Contract. Deliverable is also used in a more informal way to mean a planned output of any Process.
Demand Management	Activities that understand and influence Customer demand for Services and the provision of Capacity to meet these demands. At a Strategic level Demand Management can involve analysis of Patterns of Business Activity and User Profiles. At a Tactical level it can involve use of Differential Charging to encourage Customers to use IT Services at less busy times. See Capacity Management.
Deming Cycle	Synonym for Plan Do Check Act.
Dependency	The direct or indirect reliance of one Process or Activity upon another.
Deployment	(Service Transition) The Activity responsible for movement of new or changed hardware, software, documentation, Process, etc to the Live Environment. Deployment is part of the Release and Deployment Management Process. See Rollout.
Depreciation	(Service Strategy) A measure of the reduction in value of an Asset over its life. This is based on wearing out, consumption or other reduction in the useful economic value.
Design	(Service Design) An Activity or Process that identifies Requirements and then defines a solution that is able to meet these Requirements. See Service Design.
Detection	(Service Operation) A stage in the Incident Lifecycle. Detection results in the Incident becoming known to the Service Provider. Detection can be automatic, or can be the result of a User logging an Incident.

Development	(Service Design) The Process responsible for creating or modifying an IT Service or Application. Also used to mean the Role or group that carries out Development work.
Development Environment	(Service Design) An Environment used to create or modify IT Services or Applications. Development Environments are not typically subjected to the same degree of control as Test Environments or Live Environments. See Development.
Diagnosis	(Service Operation) A stage in the Incident and Problem Lifecycles. The purpose of Diagnosis is to identify a Workaround for an Incident or the Root Cause of a Problem.
Diagnostic Script	(Service Operation) A structured set of questions used by Service Desk staff to ensure they ask the correct questions, and to help them Classify, Resolve and assign Incidents. Diagnostic Scripts may also be made available to Users to help them diagnose and resolve their own Incidents.
Differential Charging	A technique used to support Demand Management by charging different amounts for the same IT Service Function at different times.
Direct Cost	(Service Strategy) A cost of providing an IT Service which can be allocated in full to a specific Customer, Cost Centre, Project etc. For example cost of providing non-shared servers or software licenses. See Indirect Cost.
Directory Service	(Service Operation) An Application that manages information about IT Infrastructure available on a network, and corresponding User access Rights.
Do Nothing	(Service Design) A Recovery Option. The Service Provider formally agrees with the Customer that Recovery of this IT Service will not be performed.
Document	Information in readable form. A Document may be paper or electronic. For example a Policy statement, Service Level Agreement, Incident Record, diagram of computer room layout. See Record.
Downtime	(Service Design) (Service Operation) The time when a Configuration Item or IT Service is not Available during its Agreed Service Time. The Availability of an IT Service is often calculated from Agreed Service Time and Downtime.
Driver	Something that influences Strategy, Objectives or Requirements. For example new legislation or the actions of competitors.
Early Life Support	(Service Transition) Support provided for a new or Changed IT Service for a period of time after it is Released. During Early Life Support the IT Service Provider may review the KPIs, Service Levels and Monitoring Thresholds, and provide additional Resources for Incident and Problem Management.
Economies of scale	(Service Strategy) The reduction in average Cost that is possible from increasing the usage of an IT Service or Asset. See Economies of Scope.

Economies of scope	(Service Strategy) The reduction in Cost that is allocated to an IT Service by using an existing Asset for an additional purpose. For example delivering a new IT Service from existing IT Infrastructure. See Economies of Scale.
Effectiveness	(Continual Service Improvement) A measure of whether the Objectives of a Process, Service or Activity have been achieved. An Effective Process or Activity is one that achieves its agreed Objectives. See KPI.
Efficiency	(Continual Service Improvement) A measure of whether the right amount of resources have been used to deliver a Process, Service or Activity. An Efficient Process achieves its Objectives with the minimum amount of time, money, people or other resources. See KPI.
Emergency Change	(Service Transition) A Change that must be introduced as soon as possible. For example to resolve a Major Incident or implement a Security patch. The Change Management Process will normally have a specific Procedure for handling Emergency Changes. See Emergency Change Advisory Board (ECAB).
Emergency Change Advisory Board (ECAB)	(Service Transition) A sub-set of the Change Advisory Board who make decisions about high impact Emergency Changes. Membership of the ECAB may be decided at the time a meeting is called, and depends on the nature of the Emergency Change.
Environment	(Service Transition) A subset of the IT Infrastructure that is used for a particular purpose. For Example: Live Environment, Test Environment, Build Environment. It is possible for multiple Environments to share a Configuration Item, for example Test and Live Environments may use different partitions on a single mainframe computer. Also used in the term Physical Environment to mean the accommodation, air conditioning, power system etc. Environment is also used as a generic term to mean the external conditions that influence or affect something.
Error	(Service Operation) A design flaw or malfunction that causes a Failure of one or more Configuration Items or IT Services. A mistake made by a person or a faulty Process that impacts a CI or IT Service is also an Error.
Escalation	(Service Operation) An Activity that obtains additional Resources when these are needed to meet Service Level Targets or Customer expectations. Escalation may be needed within any IT Service Management Process, but is most commonly associated with Incident Management, Problem Management and the management of Customer complaints. There are two types of Escalation, Functional Escalation and Hierarchic Escalation.

eSourcing Capability Model for Client Organizations (eSCM-CL)	(Service Strategy) A framework to help Organizations guide their analysis and decisions on Service Sourcing Models and Strategies. eSCM-CL was developed by Carnegie Mellon University. See eSCM-SP.
eSourcing Capability Model for Service Providers (eSCM-SP)	(Service Strategy) A framework to help IT Service Providers develop their IT Service Management Capabilities from a Service Sourcing perspective. eSCM-SP was developed by Carnegie Mellon University. See eSCM-CL.
Estimation	The use of experience to provide an approximate value for a Metric or Cost. Estimation is also used in Capacity and Availability Management as the cheapest and least accurate Modeling method.
Evaluation	(Service Transition) The Process responsible for assessing a new or Changed IT Service to ensure that Risks have been managed and to help determine whether to proceed with the Change. Evaluation is also used to mean comparing an actual Outcome with the intended Outcome, or comparing one alternative with another.
Event	(Service Operation) A change of state which has significance for the management of a Configuration Item or IT Service. The term Event is also used to mean an Alert or notification created by any IT Service, Configuration Item or Monitoring tool. Events typically require IT Operations personnel to take actions, and often lead to Incidents being logged.
Event Management	(Service Operation) The Process responsible for managing Events throughout their Lifecycle. Event Management is one of the main Activities of IT Operations.
Exception Report	A Document containing details of one or more KPIs or other important targets that have exceeded defined Thresholds. Examples include SLA targets being missed or about to be missed, and a Performance Metric indicating a potential Capacity problem.
Expanded Incident Lifecycle	(Availability Management) Detailed stages in the Lifecycle of an Incident. The stages are Detection, Diagnosis, Repair, Recovery, Restoration. The Expanded Incident Lifecycle is used to help understand all contributions to the Impact of Incidents and to Plan how these could be controlled or reduced.
External Customer	A Customer who works for a different Business to the IT Service Provider. See External Service Provider, Internal Customer.
External Metric	A Metric that is used to measure the delivery of IT Service to a Customer. External Metrics are usually defined in SLAs and reported to Customers. See Internal Metric.
External Service Provider	(Service Strategy) An IT Service Provider which is part of a different Organization to their Customer. An IT Service Provider may have both Internal Customers and External Customers. See Type III Service Provider.

External Sourcing	Synonym for Outsourcing.
Facilities Management	(Service Operation) The Function responsible for managing the physical Environment where the IT Infrastructure is located. Facilities Management includes all aspects of managing the physical Environment, for example power and cooling, building Access Management, and environmental Monitoring.
Failure	(Service Operation) Loss of ability to Operate to Specification, or to deliver the required output. The term Failure may be used when referring to IT Services, Processes, Activities, Configuration Items etc. A Failure often causes an Incident.
Failure Modes and Effects Analysis (FMEA)	An approach to assessing the potential Impact of Failures. FMEA involves analyzing what would happen after Failure of each Configuration Item, all the way up to the effect on the Business. FMEA is often used in Information Security Management and in IT Service Continuity Planning.
Fast Recovery	(Service Design) A Recovery Option which is also known as Hot Standby. Provision is made to Recover the IT Service in a short period of time, typically less than 24 hours. Fast Recovery typically uses a dedicated Fixed Facility with computer Systems, and software configured ready to run the IT Services. Immediate Recovery may take up to 24 hours if there is a need to Restore data from Backups.
Fault	Synonym for Error.
Fault Tolerance	(Service Design) The ability of an IT Service or Configuration Item to continue to Operate correctly after Failure of a Component part. See Resilience, Countermeasure.
Fault Tree Analysis (FTA)	(Service Design) (Continual Service Improvement) A technique that can be used to determine the chain of Events that leads to a Problem. Fault Tree Analysis represents a chain of Events using Boolean notation in a diagram.
Financial Management	(Service Strategy) The Function and Processes responsible for managing an IT Service Provider's Budgeting, Accounting and Charging Requirements.
First-line Support	(Service Operation) The first level in a hierarchy of Support Groups involved in the resolution of Incidents. Each level contains more specialist skills, or has more time or other Resources. See Escalation.
Fishbone Diagram	Synonym for Ishikawa Diagram.
Fit for Purpose	An informal term used to describe a Process, Configuration Item, IT Service etc. that is capable of meeting its Objectives or Service Levels. Being Fit for Purpose requires suitable Design, implementation, Control and maintenance.
Fixed Cost	(Service Strategy) A Cost that does not vary with IT Service usage. For example the cost of Server hardware. See Variable Cost.

Fixed Facility   (Service Design) A permanent building, available for use when needed by an IT
                                  Service Continuity Plan.
                                  See Recovery Option, Portable Facility.

Follow the Sun   (Service Operation) A methodology for using Service Desks and Support Groups
                                  around the world to provide seamless 24 * 7 Service. Calls, Incidents, Problems and
                                  Service Requests are passed between groups in different time zones.

Fulfilment   Performing Activities to meet a need or Requirement. For example by providing a
                                  new IT Service, or meeting a Service Request.

Function   A team or group of people and the tools they use to carry out one or more
                                  Processes or Activities. For example the Service Desk.
                                  The term Function also has two other meanings
                                  •   An intended purpose of a Configuration Item, Person, Team, Process, or
                                       IT Service. For example one Function of an Email Service may be to store
                                       and forward outgoing mails, one Function of a Business Process may be to
                                       dispatch goods to Customers.
                                  •   To perform the intended purpose correctly, "The computer is Functioning"

Functional Escalation   (Service Operation) Transferring an Incident, Problem or Change to a technical
                                  team with a higher level of expertise to assist in an Escalation.

Gap Analysis   (Continual Service Improvement) An Activity which compares two sets of data
                                  and identifies the differences. Gap Analysis is commonly used to compare a set of
                                  Requirements with actual delivery.
                                  See Benchmarking.

Governance   Ensuring that Policies and Strategy are actually implemented, and that required
                                  Processes are correctly followed. Governance includes defining Roles and
                                  responsibilities, measuring and reporting, and taking actions to resolve any issues
                                  identified.

Gradual Recovery   (Service Design) A Recovery Option which is also known as Cold Standby.
                                  Provision is made to Recover the IT Service in a period of time greater than
                                  72 hours. Gradual Recovery typically uses a Portable or Fixed Facility that has
                                  environmental support and network cabling, but no computer Systems. The
                                  hardware and software are installed as part of the IT Service Continuity Plan.

Guideline   A Document describing Best Practice, that recommends what should be done.
                                  Compliance to a guideline is not normally enforced.
                                  See Standard.

Help Desk   (Service Operation) A point of contact for Users to log Incidents. A Help Desk
                                  is usually more technically focused than a Service Desk and does not provide a
                                  Single Point of Contact for all interaction. The term Help Desk is often used as a
                                  synonym for Service Desk.

Hierarchic Escalation   (Service Operation) Informing or involving more senior levels of management to
                                  assist in an Escalation.

High Availability	(Service Design) An approach or Design that minimizes or hides the effects of Configuration Item Failure on the Users of an IT Service. High Availability solutions are Designed to achieve an agreed level of Availability and make use of techniques such as Fault Tolerance, Resilience and fast Recovery to reduce the number of Incidents, and the Impact of Incidents.
Hot Standby	Synonym for Fast Recovery or Immediate Recovery.
Identity	(Service Operation) A unique name that is used to identify a User, person or Role. The Identity is used to grant Rights to that User, person, or Role. Example identities might be the username SmithJ or the Role "Change manager".
Immediate Recovery	(Service Design) A Recovery Option which is also known as Hot Standby. Provision is made to Recover the IT Service with no loss of Service. Immediate Recovery typically uses mirroring, load balancing and split site technologies.
Impact	(Service Operation) (Service Transition) A measure of the effect of an Incident, Problem or Change on Business Processes. Impact is often based on how Service Levels will be affected. Impact and Urgency are used to assign Priority.
Incident	(Service Operation) An unplanned interruption to an IT Service or a reduction in the Quality of an IT Service. Failure of a Configuration Item that has not yet impacted Service is also an Incident. For example Failure of one disk from a mirror set.
Incident Management	(Service Operation) The Process responsible for managing the Lifecycle of all Incidents. The primary Objective of Incident Management is to return the IT Service to Users as quickly as possible.
Incident Record	(Service Operation) A Record containing the details of an Incident. Each Incident record documents the Lifecycle of a single Incident.
Indirect Cost	(Service Strategy) A Cost of providing an IT Service which cannot be allocated in full to a specific Customer. For example Cost of providing shared Servers or software licenses. Also known as Overhead. See Direct Cost.
Information Security Management (ISM)	(Service Design) The Process that ensures the Confidentiality, Integrity and Availability of an Organization's Assets, information, data and IT Services. Information Security Management usually forms part of an Organizational approach to Security Management which has a wider scope than the IT Service Provider, and includes handling of paper, building access, phone calls etc., for the entire Organization.
Information Security Management System (ISMS)	(Service Design) The framework of Policy, Processes, Standards, Guidelines and tools that ensures an Organization can achieve its Information Security Management Objectives.
Information Security Policy	(Service Design) The Policy that governs the Organization's approach to Information Security Management.

Information Technology (IT)	The use of technology for the storage, communication or processing of information. The technology typically includes computers, telecommunications, Applications and other software. The information may include Business data, voice, images, video, etc. Information Technology is often used to support Business Processes through IT Services.
Infrastructure Service	An IT Service that is not directly used by the Business, but is required by the IT Service Provider so they can provide other IT Services. For example Directory Services, naming services, or communication services.
Insourcing	Synonym for Internal Sourcing.
Integrity	(Service Design) A security principle that ensures data and Configuration Items are only modified by authorized personnel and Activities. Integrity considers all possible causes of modification, including software and hardware Failure, environmental Events, and human intervention.
Interactive Voice Response (IVR)	(Service Operation) A form of Automatic Call Distribution that accepts User input, such as key presses and spoken commands, to identify the correct destination for incoming Calls.
Intermediate Recovery	(Service Design) A Recovery Option which is also known as Warm Standby. Provision is made to Recover the IT Service in a period of time between 24 and 72 hours. Intermediate Recovery typically uses a shared Portable or Fixed Facility that has computer Systems and network Components. The hardware and software will need to be configured, and data will need to be restored, as part of the IT Service Continuity Plan.
Internal Customer	A Customer who works for the same Business as the IT Service Provider. See Internal Service Provider, External Customer.
Internal Metric	A Metric that is used within the IT Service Provider to Monitor the Efficiency, Effectiveness or Cost Effectiveness of the IT Service Provider's internal Processes. Internal Metrics are not normally reported to the Customer of the IT Service. See External Metric.
Internal Rate of Return (IRR)	(Service Strategy) A technique used to help make decisions about Capital Expenditure. IRR calculates a figure that allows two or more alternative investments to be compared. A larger IRR indicates a better investment. See Net Present Value, Return on Investment.
Internal Service Provider	(Service Strategy) An IT Service Provider which is part of the same Organization as their Customer. An IT Service Provider may have both Internal Customers and External Customers. See Type I Service Provider, Type II Service Provider, Insource.
Internal Sourcing	(Service Strategy) Using an Internal Service Provider to manage IT Services. See Service Sourcing, Type I Service Provider, Type II Service Provider.

International Organization for Standardization (ISO)	The International Organization for Standardization (ISO) is the world's largest developer of Standards. ISO is a non-governmental organization which is a network of the national standards institutes of 156 countries. Further information about ISO is available from http://www.iso.org/
International Standards Organization	See International Organization for Standardization (ISO)
Internet Service Provider (ISP)	An External Service Provider that provides access to the Internet. Most ISPs also provide other IT Services such as web hosting.
Invocation	(Service Design) Initiation of the steps defined in a plan. For example initiating the IT Service Continuity Plan for one or more IT Services.
Ishikawa Diagram	(Service Operation) (Continual Service Improvement) A technique that helps a team to identify all the possible causes of a Problem. Originally devised by Kaoru Ishikawa, the output of this technique is a diagram that looks like a fishbone.
ISO 9000	A generic term that refers to a number of international Standards and Guidelines for Quality Management Systems. See http://www.iso.org/ for more information. See ISO.
ISO 9001	An international Standard for Quality Management Systems. See ISO 9000, Standard.
ISO/IEC 17799	(Continual Service Improvement) ISO Code of Practice for Information Security Management. See Standard.
ISO/IEC 20000	ISO Specification and Code of Practice for IT Service Management. ISO/IEC 20000 is aligned with ITIL Best Practice.
ISO/IEC 27001	(Service Design) (Continual Service Improvement) ISO Specification for Information Security Management. The corresponding Code of Practice is ISO/IEC 17799. See Standard.
IT Directorate	(Continual Service Improvement) Senior Management within a Service Provider, charged with developing and delivering IT services. Most commonly used in UK Government departments.
IT Infrastructure	All of the hardware, software, networks, facilities etc. that are required to Develop, Test, deliver, Monitor, Control or support IT Services. The term IT Infrastructure includes all of the Information Technology but not the associated people, Processes and documentation.
IT Operations	(Service Operation) Activities carried out by IT Operations Control, including Console Management, Job Scheduling, Backup and Restore, and Print and Output Management. IT Operations is also used as a synonym for Service Operation.

IT Operations Control	(Service Operation) The Function responsible for Monitoring and Control of the IT Services and IT Infrastructure. See Operations Bridge.
IT Operations Management	(Service Operation) The Function within an IT Service Provider which performs the daily Activities needed to manage IT Services and the supporting IT Infrastructure. IT Operations Management includes IT Operations Control and Facilities Management.
IT Service	A Service provided to one or more Customers by an IT Service Provider. An IT Service is based on the use of Information Technology and supports the Customer's Business Processes. An IT Service is made up from a combination of people, Processes and technology and should be defined in a Service Level Agreement.
IT Service Continuity Management (ITSCM)	(Service Design) The Process responsible for managing Risks that could seriously impact IT Services. ITSCM ensures that the IT Service Provider can always provide minimum agreed Service Levels, by reducing the Risk to an acceptable level and Planning for the Recovery of IT Services. ITSCM should be designed to support Business Continuity Management.
IT Service Continuity Plan	(Service Design) A Plan defining the steps required to Recover one or more IT Services. The Plan will also identify the triggers for Invocation, people to be involved, communications etc. The IT Service Continuity Plan should be part of a Business Continuity Plan.
IT Service Management (ITSM)	The implementation and management of Quality IT Services that meet the needs of the Business. IT Service Management is performed by IT Service Providers through an appropriate mix of people, Process and Information Technology. See Service Management.
IT Service Management Forum (itSMF)	The IT Service Management Forum is an independent Organization dedicated to promoting a professional approach to IT Service Management. The itSMF is a not-for-profit membership Organization with representation in many countries around the world (itSMF Chapters). The itSMF and its membership contribute to the development of ITIL and associated IT Service Management Standards. See http://www.itsmf.com/ for more information.
IT Service Provider	(Service Strategy) A Service Provider that provides IT Services to Internal Customers or External Customers.
IT Steering Group (ISG)	A formal group that is responsible for ensuring that Business and IT Service Provider Strategies and Plans are closely aligned. An IT Steering Group includes senior representatives from the Business and the IT Service Provider.
ITIL	A set of Best Practice guidance for IT Service Management. ITIL is owned by the OGC and consists of a series of publications giving guidance on the provision of Quality IT Services, and on the Processes and facilities needed to support them. See http://www.itil.co.uk/ for more information.

Job Description	A Document which defines the Roles, responsibilities, skills and knowledge required by a particular person. One Job Description can include multiple Roles, for example the Roles of Configuration Manager and Change Manager may be carried out by one person.
Job Scheduling	(Service Operation) Planning and managing the execution of software tasks that are required as part of an IT Service. Job Scheduling is carried out by IT Operations Management, and is often automated using software tools that run batch or online tasks at specific times of the day, week, month or year.
Kano Model	(Service Strategy) A Model developed by Noriaki Kano that is used to help understand Customer preferences. The Kano Model considers Attributes of an IT Service grouped into areas such as Basic Factors, Excitement Factors, Performance Factors etc.
Kepner & Tregoe Analysis	(Service Operation) (Continual Service Improvement) A structured approach to Problem solving. The Problem is analyzed in terms of what, where, when and extent. Possible causes are identified. The most probable cause is tested. The true cause is verified.
Key Performance Indicator (KPI)	(Continual Service Improvement) A Metric that is used to help manage a Process, IT Service or Activity. Many Metrics may be measured, but only the most important of these are defined as KPIs and used to actively manage and report on the Process, IT Service or Activity. KPIs should be selected to ensure that Efficiency, Effectiveness, and Cost Effectiveness are all managed. See Critical Success Factor.
Knowledge Base	(Service Transition) A logical database containing the data used by the Service Knowledge Management System.
Knowledge Management	(Service Transition) The Process responsible for gathering, analyzing, storing and sharing knowledge and information within an Organization. The primary purpose of Knowledge Management is to improve Efficiency by reducing the need to rediscover knowledge. See Data-to-Information-to-Knowledge-to-Wisdom, Service Knowledge Management System.
Known Error	(Service Operation) A Problem that has a documented Root Cause and a Workaround. Known Errors are created and managed throughout their Lifecycle by Problem Management. Known Errors may also be identified by Development or Suppliers.
Known Error Database (KEDB)	(Service Operation) A database containing all Known Error Records. This database is created by Problem Management and used by Incident and Problem Management. The Known Error Database is part of the Service Knowledge Management System.
Known Error Record	(Service Operation) A Record containing the details of a Known Error. Each Known Error Record documents the Lifecycle of a Known Error, including the Status, Root Cause and Workaround. In some implementations a Known Error is documented using additional fields in a Problem Record.

Lifecycle	The various stages in the life of an IT Service, Configuration Item, Incident, Problem, Change etc. The Lifecycle defines the Categories for Status and the Status transitions that are permitted. For example:

- The Lifecycle of an Application includes Requirements, Design, Build, Deploy, Operate, Optimize.
- The Expanded Incident Lifecycle includes Detect, Respond, Diagnose, Repair, Recover, Restore.
- The lifecycle of a Server may include: Ordered, Received, In Test, Live, Disposed etc.

Line of Service (LOS)	(Service Strategy) A Core Service or Supporting Service that has multiple Service Level Packages. A line of Service is managed by a Product Manager and each Service Level Package is designed to support a particular market segment.
Live	(Service Transition) Refers to an IT Service or Configuration Item that is being used to deliver Service to a Customer.
Live Environment	(Service Transition) A controlled Environment containing Live Configuration Items used to deliver IT Services to Customers.
Maintainability	(Service Design) A measure of how quickly and Effectively a Configuration Item or IT Service can be restored to normal working after a Failure. Maintainability is often measured and reported as MTRS. Maintainability is also used in the context of Software or IT Service Development to mean ability to be Changed or Repaired easily.
Major Incident	(Service Operation) The highest Category of Impact for an Incident. A Major Incident results in significant disruption to the Business.
Managed Services	(Service Strategy) A perspective on IT Services which emphasizes the fact that they are managed. The term Managed Services is also used as a synonym for Outsourced IT Services.
Management Information	Information that is used to support decision making by managers. Management Information is often generated automatically by tools supporting the various IT Service Management Processes. Management Information often includes the values of KPIs such as "Percentage of Changes leading to Incidents", or "first time fix rate".
Management of Risk (MoR)	The OGC methodology for managing Risks. MoR includes all the Activities required to identify and Control the exposure to Risk which may have an impact on the achievement of an Organization's Business Objectives. See http://www.m-o-r.org/ for more details.
Management System	The framework of Policy, Processes and Functions that ensures an Organization can achieve its Objectives.
Manual Workaround	A Workaround that requires manual intervention. Manual Workaround is also used as the name of a Recovery Option in which The Business Process Operates without the use of IT Services. This is a temporary measure and is usually combined with another Recovery Option.

Marginal Cost	(Service Strategy) The Cost of continuing to provide the IT Service. Marginal Cost does not include investment already made, for example the cost of developing new software and delivering training.
Market Space	(Service Strategy) All opportunities that an IT Service Provider could exploit to meet business needs of Customers. The Market Space identifies the possible IT Services that an IT Service Provider may wish to consider delivering.
Maturity	(Continual Service Improvement) A measure of the Reliability, Efficiency and Effectiveness of a Process, Function, Organization etc. The most mature Processes and Functions are formally aligned to Business Objectives and Strategy, and are supported by a framework for continual improvement.
Maturity Level	A named level in a Maturity model such as the Carnegie Mellon Capability Maturity Model Integration.
Mean Time Between Failures (MTBF)	(Service Design) A Metric for measuring and reporting Reliability. MTBF is the average time that a Configuration Item or IT Service can perform its agreed Function without interruption. This is measured from when the CI or IT Service starts working, until it next fails.
Mean Time Between Service Incidents (MTBSI)	(Service Design) A Metric used for measuring and reporting Reliability. MTBSI is the mean time from when a System or IT Service fails, until it next fails. MTBSI is equal to MTBF + MTRS.
Mean Time To Repair (MTTR)	The average time taken to repair a Configuration Item or IT Service after a Failure. MTTR is measured from when the CI or IT Service fails until it is Repaired. MTTR does not include the time required to Recover or Restore. MTTR is sometimes incorrectly used to mean Mean Time to Restore Service.
Mean Time to Restore Service (MTRS)	The average time taken to Restore a Configuration Item or IT Service after a Failure. MTRS is measured from when the CI or IT Service fails until it is fully Restored and delivering its normal functionality. See Maintainability, Mean Time to Repair.
Metric	(Continual Service Improvement) Something that is measured and reported to help manage a Process, IT Service or Activity. See KPI.
Middleware	(Service Design) Software that connects two or more software Components or Applications. Middleware is usually purchased from a Supplier, rather than developed within the IT Service Provider. See Off the Shelf.
Mission Statement	The Mission Statement of an Organization is a short but complete description of the overall purpose and intentions of that Organization. It states what is to be achieved, but not how this should be done.
Model	A representation of a System, Process, IT Service, Configuration Item etc. that is used to help understand or predict future behavior.

Modeling	A technique that is used to predict the future behavior of a System, Process, IT Service, Configuration Item etc. Modeling is commonly used in Financial Management, Capacity Management and Availability Management.
Monitor Control Loop	(Service Operation) Monitoring the output of a Task, Process, IT Service or Configuration Item; comparing this output to a predefined norm; and taking appropriate action based on this comparison.
Monitoring	(Service Operation) Repeated observation of a Configuration Item, IT Service or Process to detect Events and to ensure that the current status is known.
Near-Shore	(Service Strategy) Provision of Services from a country near the country where the Customer is based. This can be the provision of an IT Service, or of supporting Functions such as Service Desk. See On-shore, Off-shore.
Net Present Value (NPV)	(Service Strategy) A technique used to help make decisions about Capital Expenditure. NPV compares cash inflows to cash outflows. Positive NPV indicates that an investment is worthwhile. See Internal Rate of Return, Return on Investment.
Notional Charging	(Service Strategy) An approach to Charging for IT Services. Charges to Customers are calculated and Customers are informed of the charge, but no money is actually transferred. Notional Charging is sometimes introduced to ensure that Customers are aware of the Costs they incur, or as a stage during the introduction of real Charging.
Objective	The defined purpose or aim of a Process, an Activity or an Organization as a whole. Objectives are usually expressed as measurable targets. The term Objective is also informally used to mean a Requirement. See Outcome.
Off the Shelf	Synonym for Commercial Off the Shelf.
Office of Government Commerce (OGC)	OGC owns the ITIL brand (copyright and trademark). OGC is a UK Government department that supports the delivery of the government's procurement agenda through its work in collaborative procurement and in raising levels of procurement skills and capability with departments. It also provides support for complex public sector projects.
Office of Public Sector Information (OPSI)	OPSI license the Crown Copyright material used in the ITIL publications. They are a UK Government department who provide online access to UK legislation, license the re-use of Crown copyright material, manage the Information Fair Trader Scheme, maintain the Government's Information Asset Register and provide advice and guidance on official publishing and Crown copyright.
Off-shore	(Service Strategy) Provision of Services from a location outside the country where the Customer is based, often in a different continent. This can be the provision of an IT Service, or of supporting Functions such as Service Desk. See On-shore, Near-shore.

On-shore	(Service Strategy) Provision of Services from a location within the country where the Customer is based. See Off-shore, Near-shore.
Operate	To perform as expected. A Process or Configuration Item is said to Operate if it is delivering the Required outputs. Operate also means to perform one or more Operations. For example, to Operate a computer is to do the day-to-day Operations needed for it to perform as expected.
Operation	(Service Operation) Day-to-day management of an IT Service, System, or other Configuration Item. Operation is also used to mean any pre-defined Activity or Transaction. For example loading a magnetic tape, accepting money at a point of sale, or reading data from a disk drive.
Operational	The lowest of three levels of Planning and delivery (Strategic, Tactical, Operational). Operational Activities include the day-to-day or short term Planning or delivery of a Business Process or IT Service Management Process. The term Operational is also a synonym for Live.
Operational Cost	Cost resulting from running the IT Services. Often repeating payments. For example staff costs, hardware maintenance and electricity (also known as "current expenditure" or "revenue expenditure"). See Capital Expenditure.
Operational Expenditure (OPEX)	Synonym for Operational Cost.
Operational Level Agreement (OLA)	(Service Design) (Continual Service Improvement) An Agreement between an IT Service Provider and another part of the same Organization. An OLA supports the IT Service Provider's delivery of IT Services to Customers. The OLA defines the goods or Services to be provided and the responsibilities of both parties. For example there could be an OLA • between the IT Service Provider and a procurement department to obtain hardware in agreed times • between the Service Desk and a Support Group to provide Incident Resolution in agreed times. See Service Level Agreement.
Operations Bridge	(Service Operation) A physical location where IT Services and IT Infrastructure are monitored and managed.
Operations Control	Synonym for IT Operations Control.
Operations Management	Synonym for IT Operations Management.
Opportunity Cost	(Service Strategy) A Cost that is used in deciding between investment choices. Opportunity Cost represents the revenue that would have been generated by using the Resources in a different way. For example the Opportunity Cost of purchasing a new Server may include not carrying out a Service Improvement activity that the money could have been spent on. Opportunity cost analysis is used as part of a decision making processes, but is not treated as an actual Cost in any financial statement.

Optimize	Review, Plan and request Changes, in order to obtain the maximum Efficiency and Effectiveness from a Process, Configuration Item, Application etc.
Organization	A company, legal entity or other institution. Examples of Organizations that are not companies include International Standards Organization or itSMF. The term Organization is sometimes used to refer to any entity which has People, Resources and Budgets. For example a Project or Business Unit.
Outcome	The result of carrying out an Activity; following a Process; delivering an IT Service etc. The term Outcome is used to refer to intended results, as well as to actual results. See Objective.
Outsourcing	(Service Strategy) Using an External Service Provider to manage IT Services. See Service Sourcing, Type III Service Provider.
Overhead	Synonym for Indirect cost
Pain Value Analysis	(Service Operation) A technique used to help identify the Business Impact of one or more Problems. A formula is used to calculate Pain Value based on the number of Users affected, the duration of the Downtime, the Impact on each User, and the cost to the Business (if known).
Pareto Principle	(Service Operation) A technique used to priorities Activities. The Pareto Principle says that 80% of the value of any Activity is created with 20% of the effort. Pareto Analysis is also used in Problem Management to priorities possible Problem causes for investigation.
Partnership	A relationship between two Organizations which involves working closely together for common goals or mutual benefit. The IT Service Provider should have a Partnership with the Business, and with Third Parties who are critical to the delivery of IT Services. See Value Network.
Passive Monitoring	(Service Operation) Monitoring of a Configuration Item, an IT Service or a Process that relies on an Alert or notification to discover the current status. See Active Monitoring.
Pattern of Business Activity (PBA)	(Service Strategy) A Workload profile of one or more Business Activities. Patterns of Business Activity are used to help the IT Service Provider understand and plan for different levels of Business Activity. See User Profile.
Percentage utilization	(Service Design) The amount of time that a Component is busy over a given period of time. For example, if a CPU is busy for 1800 seconds in a one hour period, its utilization is 50%
Performance	A measure of what is achieved or delivered by a System, person, team, Process, or IT Service.

Performance Anatomy	(Service Strategy) An approach to Organizational Culture that integrates, and actively manages, leadership and strategy, people development, technology enablement, performance management and innovation.
Performance Management	(Continual Service Improvement) The Process responsible for day-to-day Capacity Management Activities. These include Monitoring, Threshold detection, Performance analysis and Tuning, and implementing Changes related to Performance and Capacity.
Pilot	(Service Transition) A limited Deployment of an IT Service, a Release or a Process to the Live Environment. A Pilot is used to reduce Risk and to gain User feedback and Acceptance. See Test, Evaluation.
Plan	A detailed proposal which describes the Activities and Resources needed to achieve an Objective. For example a Plan to implement a new IT Service or Process. ISO/IEC 20000 requires a Plan for the management of each IT Service Management Process.
Plan-Do-Check-Act	(Continual Service Improvement) A four stage cycle for Process management, attributed to Edward Deming. Plan-Do-Check-Act is also called the Deming Cycle. PLAN: Design or revise Processes that support the IT Services. DO: Implement the Plan and manage the Processes. CHECK: Measure the Processes and IT Services, compare with Objectives and produce reports ACT: Plan and implement Changes to improve the Processes.
Planned Downtime	(Service Design) Agreed time when an IT Service will not be available. Planned Downtime is often used for maintenance, upgrades and testing. See Change Window, Downtime.
Planning	An Activity responsible for creating one or more Plans. For example, Capacity Planning.
PMBOK	A Project management Standard maintained and published by the Project Management Institute. PMBOK stands for Project Management Body of Knowledge. See http://www.pmi.org/ for more information. See PRINCE2.
Policy	Formally documented management expectations and intentions. Policies are used to direct decisions, and to ensure consistent and appropriate development and implementation of Processes, Standards, Roles, Activities, IT Infrastructure etc.
Portable Facility	(Service Design) A prefabricated building, or a large vehicle, provided by a Third Party and moved to a site when needed by an IT Service Continuity Plan. See Recovery Option, Fixed Facility.
Post Implementation Review (PIR)	A Review that takes place after a Change or a Project has been implemented. A PIR determines if the Change or Project was successful, and identifies opportunities for improvement.

Practice	A way of working, or a way in which work must be done. Practices can include Activities, Processes, Functions, Standards and Guidelines. See Best Practice.
Prerequisite for Success (PFS)	An Activity that needs to be completed, or a condition that needs to be met, to enable successful implementation of a Plan or Process. A PFS is often an output from one Process that is a required input to another Process.
Pricing	(Service Strategy) The Activity for establishing how much Customers will be Charged.
PRINCE2	The standard UK government methodology for Project management. See http://www.ogc.gov.uk/prince2/ for more information. See PMBOK.
Priority	(Service Transition) (Service Operation) A Category used to identify the relative importance of an Incident, Problem or Change. Priority is based on Impact and Urgency, and is used to identify required times for actions to be taken. For example the SLA may state that Priority2 Incidents must be resolved within 12 hours.
Proactive Monitoring	(Service Operation) Monitoring that looks for patterns of Events to predict possible future Failures. See Reactive Monitoring.
Proactive Problem Management	(Service Operation) Part of the Problem Management Process. The Objective of Proactive Problem Management is to identify Problems that might otherwise be missed. Proactive Problem Management analyses Incident Records, and uses data collected by other IT Service Management Processes to identify trends or significant Problems.
Problem	(Service Operation) A cause of one or more Incidents. The cause is not usually known at the time a Problem Record is created, and the Problem Management Process is responsible for further investigation.
Problem Management	(Service Operation) The Process responsible for managing the Lifecycle of all Problems. The primary Objectives of Problem Management are to prevent Incidents from happening, and to minimize the Impact of Incidents that cannot be prevented.
Problem Record	(Service Operation) A Record containing the details of a Problem. Each Problem Record documents the Lifecycle of a single Problem.
Procedure	A Document containing steps that specify how to achieve an Activity. Procedures are defined as part of Processes. See Work Instruction.
Process	A structured set of Activities designed to accomplish a specific Objective. A Process takes one or more defined inputs and turns them into defined outputs. A Process may include any of the Roles, responsibilities, tools and management Controls required to reliably deliver the outputs. A Process may define Policies, Standards, Guidelines, Activities, and Work Instructions if they are needed.

Process Control	The Activity of planning and regulating a Process, with the Objective of performing the Process in an Effective, Efficient, and consistent manner.
Process Manager	A Role responsible for Operational management of a Process. The Process Manager's responsibilities include Planning and coordination of all Activities required to carry out, monitor and report on the Process. There may be several Process Managers for one Process, for example regional Change Managers or IT Service Continuity Managers for each data centre. The Process Manager Role is often assigned to the person who carries out the Process Owner Role, but the two Roles may be separate in larger Organizations.
Process Owner	A Role responsible for ensuring that a Process is Fit for Purpose. The Process Owner's responsibilities include sponsorship, Design, Change Management and continual improvement of the Process and its Metrics. This Role is often assigned to the same person who carries out the Process Manager Role, but the two Roles may be separate in larger Organizations.
Production Environment	Synonym for Live Environment.
Profit Centre	(Service Strategy) A Business Unit which charges for Services provided. A Profit Centre can be created with the objective of making a profit, recovering Costs, or running at a loss. An IT Service Provider can be run as a Cost Centre or a Profit Centre.
pro-forma	A template, or example Document containing example data that will be replaced with the real values when these are available.
Program	A number of Projects and Activities that are planned and managed together to achieve an overall set of related Objectives and other Outcomes.
Project	A temporary Organization, with people and other Assets required to achieve an Objective or other Outcome. Each Project has a Lifecycle that typically includes initiation, Planning, execution, Closure etc. Projects are usually managed using a formal methodology such as PRINCE2.
Projected Service Outage (PSO)	(Service Transition) A Document that identifies the effect of planned Changes, maintenance Activities and Test Plans on agreed Service Levels.
PRojects IN Controlled Environments (PRINCE2)	See PRINCE2
Qualification	(Service Transition) An Activity that ensures that IT Infrastructure is appropriate, and correctly configured, to support an Application or IT Service. See Validation.

Quality	The ability of a product, Service, or Process to provide the intended value. For example, a hardware Component can be considered to be of high Quality if it performs as expected and delivers the required Reliability. Process Quality also requires an ability to monitor Effectiveness and Efficiency, and to improve them if necessary. See Quality Management System.
Quality Assurance (QA)	(Service Transition) The Process responsible for ensuring that the Quality of a product, Service or Process will provide its intended Value.
Quality Management System (QMS)	(Continual Service Improvement) The set of Processes responsible for ensuring that all work carried out by an Organization is of a suitable Quality to reliably meet Business Objectives or Service Levels. See ISO 9000.
Quick Win	(Continual Service Improvement) An improvement Activity which is expected to provide a Return on Investment in a short period of time with relatively small Cost and effort. See Pareto Principle.
RACI	(Service Design) (Continual Service Improvement) A Model used to help define Roles and Responsibilities. RACI stands for Responsible, Accountable, Consulted and Informed. See Stakeholder.
Reactive Monitoring	(Service Operation) Monitoring that takes action in response to an Event. For example submitting a batch job when the previous job completes, or logging an Incident when an Error occurs. See Proactive Monitoring.
Reciprocal Arrangement	(Service Design) A Recovery Option. An agreement between two Organizations to share resources in an emergency. For example, Computer Room space or use of a mainframe.
Record	A Document containing the results or other output from a Process or Activity. Records are evidence of the fact that an Activity took place and may be paper or electronic. For example, an Audit report, an Incident Record, or the minutes of a meeting.
Recovery	(Service Design) (Service Operation) Returning a Configuration Item or an IT Service to a working state. Recovery of an IT Service often includes recovering data to a known consistent state. After Recovery, further steps may be needed before the IT Service can be made available to the Users (Restoration).
Recovery Option	(Service Design) A Strategy for responding to an interruption to Service. Commonly used Strategies are Do Nothing, Manual Workaround, Reciprocal Arrangement, Gradual Recovery, Intermediate Recovery, Fast Recovery, Immediate Recovery. Recovery Options may make use of dedicated facilities, or Third Party facilities shared by multiple Businesses.

Recovery Point Objective (RPO)	(Service Operation) The maximum amount of data that may be lost when Service is Restored after an interruption. Recovery Point Objective is expressed as a length of time before the Failure. For example a Recovery Point Objective of one day may be supported by daily Backups, and up to 24 hours of data may be lost. Recovery Point Objectives for each IT Service should be negotiated, agreed and documented, and used as Requirements for Service Design and IT Service Continuity Plans.
Recovery Time Objective (RTO)	(Service Operation) The maximum time allowed for recovery of an IT Service following an interruption. The Service Level to be provided may be less than normal Service Level Targets. Recovery Time Objectives for each IT Service should be negotiated, agreed and documented. See Business Impact Analysis.
Redundancy	Synonym for Fault Tolerance. The term Redundant also has a generic meaning of obsolete, or no longer needed.
Relationship	A connection or interaction between two people or things. In Business Relationship Management it is the interaction between the IT Service Provider and the Business. In Configuration Management it is a link between two Configuration Items that identifies a dependency or connection between them. For example Applications may be linked to the Servers they run on, IT Services have many links to all the CIs that contribute to them.
Relationship Processes	The ISO/IEC 20000 Process group that includes Business Relationship Management and Supplier Management.
Release	(Service Transition) A collection of hardware, software, documentation, Processes or other Components required to implement one or more approved Changes to IT Services. The contents of each Release are managed, Tested, and Deployed as a single entity.
Release and Deployment Management	(Service Transition) The Process responsible for both Release Management and Deployment.
Release Identification	(Service Transition) A naming convention used to uniquely identify a Release. The Release Identification typically includes a reference to the Configuration Item and a version number. For example Microsoft Office 2003 SR2.
Release Management	(Service Transition) The Process responsible for Planning, scheduling and controlling the movement of Releases to Test and Live Environments. The primary Objective of Release Management is to ensure that the integrity of the Live Environment is protected and that the correct Components are released. Release Management is part of the Release and Deployment Management Process.
Release Process	The name used by ISO/IEC 20000 for the Process group that includes Release Management. This group does not include any other Processes. Release Process is also used as a synonym for Release Management Process.

Release Record	(Service Transition) A Record in the CMDB that defines the content of a Release. A Release Record has Relationships with all Configuration Items that are affected by the Release.
Release Unit	(Service Transition) Components of an IT Service that are normally Released together. A Release Unit typically includes sufficient Components to perform a useful Function. For example one Release Unit could be a Desktop PC, including Hardware, Software, Licenses, Documentation etc. A different Release Unit may be the complete Payroll Application, including IT Operations Procedures and User training.
Release Window	Synonym for Change Window.
Reliability	(Service Design) (Continual Service Improvement) A measure of how long a Configuration Item or IT Service can perform its agreed Function without interruption. Usually measured as MTBF or MTBSI. The term Reliability can also be used to state how likely it is that a Process, Function etc. will deliver its required outputs. See Availability.
Remediation	(Service Transition) Recovery to a known state after a failed Change or Release.
Repair	(Service Operation) The replacement or correction of a failed Configuration Item.
Request for Change (RFC)	(Service Transition) A formal proposal for a Change to be made. An RFC includes details of the proposed Change, and may be recorded on paper or electronically. The term RFC is often misused to mean a Change Record, or the Change itself.
Request Fulfilment	(Service Operation) The Process responsible for managing the Lifecycle of all Service Requests.
Requirement	(Service Design) A formal statement of what is needed. For example a Service Level Requirement, a Project Requirement or the required Deliverables for a Process. See Statement of Requirements.
Resilience	(Service Design) The ability of a Configuration Item or IT Service to resist Failure or to Recover quickly following a Failure. For example, an armored cable will resist failure when put under stress. See Fault Tolerance.
Resolution	(Service Operation) Action taken to repair the Root Cause of an Incident or Problem, or to implement a Workaround. In ISO/IEC 20000, Resolution Processes is the Process group that includes Incident and Problem Management.
Resolution Processes	The ISO/IEC 20000 Process group that includes Incident Management and Problem Management.

Resource	(Service Strategy) A generic term that includes IT Infrastructure, people, money or anything else that might help to deliver an IT Service. Resources are considered to be Assets of an Organization. See Capability, Service Asset.
Response Time	A measure of the time taken to complete an Operation or Transaction. Used in Capacity Management as a measure of IT Infrastructure Performance, and in Incident Management as a measure of the time taken to answer the phone, or to start Diagnosis.
Responsiveness	A measurement of the time taken to respond to something. This could be Response Time of a Transaction, or the speed with which an IT Service Provider responds to an Incident or Request for Change etc.
Restoration of Service	See Restore.
Restore	(Service Operation) Taking action to return an IT Service to the Users after Repair and Recovery from an Incident. This is the primary Objective of Incident Management.
Retire	(Service Transition) Permanent removal of an IT Service, or other Configuration Item, from the Live Environment. Retired is a stage in the Lifecycle of many Configuration Items.
Return on Investment (ROI)	(Service Strategy) (Continual Service Improvement) A measurement of the expected benefit of an investment. In the simplest sense it is the net profit of an investment divided by the net worth of the assets invested. See Net Present Value, Value on Investment.
Return to Normal	(Service Design) The phase of an IT Service Continuity Plan during which full normal operations are resumed. For example, if an alternate data centre has been in use, then this phase will bring the primary data centre back into operation, and restore the ability to invoke IT Service Continuity Plans again.
Review	An evaluation of a Change, Problem, Process, Project etc. Reviews are typically carried out at predefined points in the Lifecycle, and especially after Closure. The purpose of a Review is to ensure that all Deliverables have been provided, and to identify opportunities for improvement. See Post Implementation Review.
Rights	(Service Operation) Entitlements, or permissions, granted to a User or Role. For example the Right to modify particular data, or to authorize a Change.
Risk	A possible Event that could cause harm or loss, or affect the ability to achieve Objectives. A Risk is measured by the probability of a Threat, the Vulnerability of the Asset to that Threat, and the Impact it would have if it occurred.

Risk Assessment	The initial steps of Risk Management. Analyzing the value of Assets to the business, identifying Threats to those Assets, and evaluating how Vulnerable each Asset is to those Threats. Risk Assessment can be quantitative (based on numerical data) or qualitative.
Risk Management	The Process responsible for identifying, assessing and controlling Risks. See Risk Assessment.
Role	A set of responsibilities, Activities and authorities granted to a person or team. A Role is defined in a Process. One person or team may have multiple Roles, for example the Roles of Configuration Manager and Change Manager may be carried out by a single person.
Rollout	(Service Transition) Synonym for Deployment. Most often used to refer to complex or phased Deployments or Deployments to multiple locations.
Root Cause	(Service Operation) The underlying or original cause of an Incident or Problem.
Root Cause Analysis (RCA)	(Service Operation) An Activity that identifies the Root Cause of an Incident or Problem. RCA typically concentrates on IT Infrastructure failures. See Service Failure Analysis.
Running Costs	Synonym for Operational Costs
Scalability	The ability of an IT Service, Process, Configuration Item etc. to perform its agreed Function when the Workload or Scope changes.
Scope	The boundary, or extent, to which a Process, Procedure, Certification, Contract etc. applies. For example the Scope of Change Management may include all Live IT Services and related Configuration Items, the Scope of an ISO/IEC 20000 Certificate may include all IT Services delivered out of a named data centre.
Second-line Support	(Service Operation) The second level in a hierarchy of Support Groups involved in the resolution of Incidents and investigation of Problems. Each level contains more specialist skills, or has more time or other Resources.
Security	See Information Security Management
Security Management	Synonym for Information Security Management
Security Policy	Synonym for Information Security Policy
Separation of Concerns (SoC)	(Service Strategy) An approach to Designing a solution or IT Service that divides the problem into pieces that can be solved independently. This approach separates "what" is to be done from "how" it is to be done.
Server	(Service Operation) A computer that is connected to a network and provides software Functions that are used by other computers.
Service	A means of delivering value to Customers by facilitating Outcomes Customers want to achieve without the ownership of specific Costs and Risks.

Service Acceptance Criteria (SAC)	(Service Transition) A set of criteria used to ensure that an IT Service meets its functionality and Quality Requirements and that the IT Service Provider is ready to Operate the new IT Service when it has been Deployed. See Acceptance.
Service Analytics	(Service Strategy) A technique used in the Assessment of the Business Impact of Incidents. Service Analytics Models the dependencies between Configuration Items, and the dependencies of IT Services on Configuration Items.
Service Asset	Any Capability or Resource of a Service Provider. See Asset.
Service Asset and Configuration Management (SACM)	(Service Transition) The Process responsible for both Configuration Management and Asset Management.
Service Capacity Management (SCM)	(Service Design) (Continual Service Improvement) The Activity responsible for understanding the Performance and Capacity of IT Services. The Resources used by each IT Service and the pattern of usage over time are collected, recorded, and analyzed for use in the Capacity Plan. See Business Capacity Management, Component Capacity Management.
Service Catalogue	(Service Design) A database or structured Document with information about all Live IT Services, including those available for Deployment. The Service Catalogue is the only part of the Service Portfolio published to Customers, and is used to support the sale and delivery of IT Services. The Service Catalogue includes information about deliverables, prices, contact points, ordering and request Processes. See Contract Portfolio.
Service Continuity Management	Synonym for IT Service Continuity Management.
Service Contract	(Service Strategy) A Contract to deliver one or more IT Services. The term Service Contract is also used to mean any Agreement to deliver IT Services, whether this is a legal Contract or an SLA. See Contract Portfolio.
Service Culture	A Customer oriented Culture. The major Objectives of a Service Culture are Customer satisfaction and helping the Customer to achieve their Business Objectives.
Service Design	(Service Design) A stage in the Lifecycle of an IT Service. Service Design includes a number of Processes and Functions and is the title of one of the Core ITIL publications. See Design.
Service Design Package	(Service Design) Document(s) defining all aspects of an IT Service and its Requirements through each stage of its Lifecycle. A Service Design Package is produced for each new IT Service, major Change, or IT Service Retirement.

Service Desk

(Service Operation) The Single Point of Contact between the Service Provider and the Users. A typical Service Desk manages Incidents and Service Requests, and also handles communication with the Users.

Service Failure
Analysis (SFA)

(Service Design) An Activity that identifies underlying causes of one or more IT Service interruptions. SFA identifies opportunities to improve the IT Service Provider's Processes and tools, and not just the IT Infrastructure. SFA is a time constrained, project-like activity, rather than an ongoing process of analysis. See Root Cause Analysis.

Service Hours

(Service Design) (Continual Service Improvement) An agreed time period when a particular IT Service should be Available. For example, "Monday-Friday 08:00 to 17:00 except public holidays". Service Hours should be defined in a Service Level Agreement.

Service Improvement
Plan (SIP)

(Continual Service Improvement) A formal Plan to implement improvements to a Process or IT Service.

Service Knowledge
Management System
(SKMS)

(Service Transition) A set of tools and databases that are used to manage knowledge and information. The SKMS includes the Configuration Management System, as well as other tools and databases. The SKMS stores, manages, updates, and presents all information that an IT Service Provider needs to manage the full Lifecycle of IT Services.

Service Level

Measured and reported achievement against one or more Service Level Targets. The term Service Level is sometimes used informally to mean Service Level Target.

Service Level
Agreement (SLA)

(Service Design) (Continual Service Improvement) An Agreement between an IT Service Provider and a Customer. The SLA describes the IT Service, documents Service Level Targets, and specifies the responsibilities of the IT Service Provider and the Customer. A single SLA may cover multiple IT Services or multiple Customers.
See Operational Level Agreement.

Service Level
Management (SLM)

(Service Design) (Continual Service Improvement) The Process responsible for negotiating Service Level Agreements, and ensuring that these are met. SLM is responsible for ensuring that all IT Service Management Processes, Operational Level Agreements, and Underpinning Contracts, are appropriate for the agreed Service Level Targets. SLM monitors and reports on Service Levels, and holds regular Customer reviews.

Service Level
Package (SLP)

(Service Strategy) A defined level of Utility and Warranty for a particular Service Package. Each SLP is designed to meet the needs of a particular Pattern of Business Activity.
See Line of Service.

Service Level
Requirement (SLR)

(Service Design) (Continual Service Improvement) A Customer Requirement for an aspect of an IT Service. SLRs are based on Business Objectives and are used to negotiate agreed Service Level Targets.

Service Level Target	(Service Design) (Continual Service Improvement) A commitment that is documented in a Service Level Agreement. Service Level Targets are based on Service Level Requirements, and are needed to ensure that the IT Service design is Fit for Purpose. Service Level Targets should be SMART, and are usually based on KPIs.
Service Maintenance Objective	(Service Operation) The expected time that a Configuration Item will be unavailable due to planned maintenance Activity.
Service Management	Service Management is a set of specialized organizational capabilities for providing value to customers in the form of services.
Service Management Lifecycle	An approach to IT Service Management that emphasizes the importance of coordination and Control across the various Functions, Processes, and Systems necessary to manage the full Lifecycle of IT Services. The Service Management Lifecycle approach considers the Strategy, Design, Transition, Operation and Continuous Improvement of IT Services.
Service Manager	A manager who is responsible for managing the end-to-end Lifecycle of one or more IT Services. The term Service Manager is also used to mean any manager within the IT Service Provider. Most commonly used to refer to a Business Relationship Manager, a Process Manager, an Account Manager or a senior manager with responsibility for IT Services overall.
Service Operation	(Service Operation) A stage in the Lifecycle of an IT Service. Service Operation includes a number of Processes and Functions and is the title of one of the Core ITIL publications. See Operation.
Service Owner	(Continual Service Improvement) A Role which is accountable for the delivery of a specific IT Service.
Service Package	(Service Strategy) A detailed description of an IT Service that is available to be delivered to Customers. A Service Package includes a Service Level Package and one or more Core Services and Supporting Services.
Service Pipeline	(Service Strategy) A database or structured Document listing all IT Services that are under consideration or Development, but are not yet available to Customers. The Service Pipeline provides a Business view of possible future IT Services and is part of the Service Portfolio which is not normally published to Customers.
Service Portfolio	(Service Strategy) The complete set of Services that are managed by a Service Provider. The Service Portfolio is used to manage the entire Lifecycle of all Services, and includes three Categories: Service Pipeline (proposed or in Development); Service Catalogue (Live or available for Deployment); and Retired Services. See Service Portfolio Management, Contract Portfolio.
Service Portfolio Management (SPM)	(Service Strategy) The Process responsible for managing the Service Portfolio. Service Portfolio Management considers Services in terms of the Business value that they provide.

Service Potential	(Service Strategy) The total possible value of the overall Capabilities and Resources of the IT Service Provider.
Service Provider	(Service Strategy) An Organization supplying Services to one or more Internal Customers or External Customers. Service Provider is often used as an abbreviation for IT Service Provider. See Type I Service Provider, Type II Service Provider, Type III Service Provider.
Service Provider Interface (SPI)	(Service Strategy) An interface between the IT Service Provider and a User, Customer, Business Process, or a Supplier. Analysis of Service Provider Interfaces helps to coordinate end-to-end management of IT Services.
Service Provisioning Optimization (SPO)	(Service Strategy) Analyzing the finances and constraints of an IT Service to decide if alternative approaches to Service delivery might reduce Costs or improve Quality.
Service Reporting	(Continual Service Improvement) The Process responsible for producing and delivering reports of achievement and trends against Service Levels. Service Reporting should agree the format, content and frequency of reports with Customers.
Service Request	(Service Operation) A request from a User for information, or advice, or for a Standard Change or for Access to an IT Service. For example to reset a password, or to provide standard IT Services for a new User. Service Requests are usually handled by a Service Desk, and do not require an RFC to be submitted. See Request Fulfilment.
Service Sourcing	(Service Strategy) The Strategy and approach for deciding whether to provide a Service internally or to Outsource it to an External Service Provider. Service Sourcing also means the execution of this Strategy. Service Sourcing includes: <ul><li>Internal Sourcing - Internal or Shared Services using Type I or Type II Service Providers.</li><li>Traditional Sourcing - Full Service Outsourcing using a Type III Service Provider.</li><li>Multivendor Sourcing - Prime, Consortium or Selective Outsourcing using Type III Service Providers.</li></ul>
Service Strategy	(Service Strategy) The title of one of the Core ITIL publications. Service Strategy establishes an overall Strategy for IT Services and for IT Service Management.
Service Transition	(Service Transition) A stage in the Lifecycle of an IT Service. Service Transition includes a number of Processes and Functions and is the title of one of the Core ITIL publications. See Transition.
Service Utility	(Service Strategy) The Functionality of an IT Service from the Customer's perspective. The Business value of an IT Service is created by the combination of Service Utility (what the Service does) and Service Warranty (how well it does it). See Utility.

Service Validation and Testing	(Service Transition) The Process responsible for Validation and Testing of a new or Changed IT Service. Service Validation and Testing ensures that the IT Service matches its Design Specification and will meet the needs of the Business.
Service Valuation	(Service Strategy) A measurement of the total Cost of delivering an IT Service, and the total value to the Business of that IT Service. Service Valuation is used to help the Business and the IT Service Provider agree on the value of the IT Service.
Service Warranty	(Service Strategy) Assurance that an IT Service will meet agreed Requirements. This may be a formal Agreement such as a Service Level Agreement or Contract, or may be a marketing message or brand image. The Business value of an IT Service is created by the combination of Service Utility (what the Service does) and Service Warranty (how well it does it). See Warranty.
Serviceability	(Service Design) (Continual Service Improvement) The ability of a Third Party Supplier to meet the terms of their Contract. This Contract will include agreed levels of Reliability, Maintainability or Availability for a Configuration Item.
Shift	(Service Operation) A group or team of people who carry out a specific Role for a fixed period of time. For example there could be four shifts of IT Operations Control personnel to support an IT Service that is used 24 hours a day.
Simulation modeling	(Service Design) (Continual Service Improvement) A technique that creates a detailed Model to predict the behavior of a Configuration Item or IT Service. Simulation Models can be very accurate but are expensive and time consuming to create. A Simulation Model is often created by using the actual Configuration Items that are being modeled, with artificial Workloads or Transactions. They are used in Capacity Management when accurate results are important. A simulation model is sometimes called a Performance Benchmark.
Single Point of Contact	(Service Operation) Providing a single consistent way to communicate with an Organization or Business Unit. For example, a Single Point of Contact for an IT Service Provider is usually called a Service Desk.
Single Point of Failure (SPOF)	(Service Design) Any Configuration Item that can cause an Incident when it fails, and for which a Countermeasure has not been implemented. A SPOF may be a person, or a step in a Process or Activity, as well as a Component of the IT Infrastructure. See Failure.
SLAM Chart	(Continual Service Improvement) A Service Level Agreement Monitoring Chart is used to help monitor and report achievements against Service Level Targets. A SLAM Chart is typically color coded to show whether each agreed Service Level Target has been met, missed, or nearly missed during each of the previous 12 months.
SMART	(Service Design) (Continual Service Improvement) An acronym for helping to remember that targets in Service Level Agreements and Project Plans should be Specific, Measurable, Achievable, Relevant and Timely.

Snapshot	(Service Transition) The current state of a Configuration as captured by a discovery tool. Also used as a synonym for Benchmark. See Baseline.
Source	See Service Sourcing.
Specification	A formal definition of Requirements. A Specification may be used to define technical or Operational Requirements, and may be internal or external. Many public Standards consist of a Code of Practice and a Specification. The Specification defines the Standard against which an Organization can be Audited.
Stakeholder	All people who have an interest in an Organization, Project, IT Service etc. Stakeholders may be interested in the Activities, targets, Resources, or Deliverables. Stakeholders may include Customers, Partners, employees, shareholders, owners, etc. See RACI.
Standard	A mandatory Requirement. Examples include ISO/IEC 20000 (an international Standard), an internal security Standard for Unix configuration, or a government Standard for how financial Records should be maintained. The term Standard is also used to refer to a Code of Practice or Specification published by a Standards Organization such as ISO or BSI. See Guideline.
Standard Change	(Service Transition) A pre-approved Change that is low Risk, relatively common and follows a Procedure or Work Instruction. For example password reset or provision of standard equipment to a new employee. RFCs are not required to implement a Standard Change, and they are logged and tracked using a different mechanism, such as a Service Request. See Change Model.
Standard Operating Procedures (SOP)	(Service Operation) Procedures used by IT Operations Management.
Standby	(Service Design) Used to refer to Resources that are not required to deliver the Live IT Services, but are available to support IT Service Continuity Plans. For example a Standby data centre may be maintained to support Hot Standby, Warm Standby or Cold Standby arrangements.
Statement of requirements (SOR)	(Service Design) A Document containing all Requirements for a product purchase, or a new or changed IT Service. See Terms of Reference.
Status	The name of a required field in many types of Record. It shows the current stage in the Lifecycle of the associated Configuration Item, Incident, Problem etc.
Status Accounting	(Service Transition) The Activity responsible for recording and reporting the Lifecycle of each Configuration Item.

Storage Management	(Service Operation) The Process responsible for managing the storage and maintenance of data throughout its Lifecycle.
Strategic	(Service Strategy) The highest of three levels of Planning and delivery (Strategic, Tactical, Operational). Strategic Activities include Objective setting and long term Planning to achieve the overall Vision.
Strategy	(Service Strategy) A Strategic Plan designed to achieve defined Objectives.
Super User	(Service Operation) A User who helps other Users, and assists in communication with the Service Desk or other parts of the IT Service Provider. Super Users typically provide support for minor Incidents and training.
Supplier	(Service Strategy) (Service Design) A Third Party responsible for supplying goods or Services that are required to deliver IT services. Examples of suppliers include commodity hardware and software vendors, network and telecom providers, and Outsourcing Organizations. See Underpinning Contract, Supply Chain.
Supplier and Contract Database (SCD)	(Service Design) A database or structured Document used to manage Supplier Contracts throughout their Lifecycle. The SCD contains key Attributes of all Contracts with Suppliers, and should be part of the Service Knowledge Management System.
Supplier Management	(Service Design) The Process responsible for ensuring that all Contracts with Suppliers support the needs of the Business, and that all Suppliers meet their contractual commitments.
Supply Chain	(Service Strategy) The Activities in a Value Chain carried out by Suppliers. A Supply Chain typically involves multiple Suppliers, each adding value to the product or Service. See Value Network.
Support Group	(Service Operation) A group of people with technical skills. Support Groups provide the Technical Support needed by all of the IT Service Management Processes. See Technical Management.
Support Hours	(Service Design) (Service Operation) The times or hours when support is available to the Users. Typically this is the hours when the Service Desk is available. Support Hours should be defined in a Service Level Agreement, and may be different from Service Hours. For example, Service Hours may be 24 hours a day, but the Support Hours may be 07:00 to 19:00.
Supporting Service	(Service Strategy) A Service that enables or enhances a Core Service. For example a Directory Service or a Backup Service. See Service Package.
SWOT Analysis	(Continual Service Improvement) A technique that reviews and analyses the internal strengths and weaknesses of an Organization and the external opportunities and threats which it faces SWOT stands for Strengths, Weaknesses, Opportunities and Threats.

System	A number of related things that work together to achieve an overall Objective. For example:
	• A computer System including hardware, software and Applications.
	• A management System, including multiple Processes that are planned and managed together. For example a Quality Management System.
	• A Database Management System or Operating System that includes many software modules that are designed to perform a set of related Functions.
System Management	The part of IT Service Management that focuses on the management of IT Infrastructure rather than Process.
Tactical	The middle of three levels of Planning and delivery (Strategic, Tactical, Operational). Tactical Activities include the medium term Plans required to achieve specific Objectives, typically over a period of weeks to months.
Tag	(Service Strategy) A short code used to identify a Category. For example tags EC1, EC2, EC3 etc. might be used to identify different Customer outcomes when analyzing and comparing Strategies. The term Tag is also used to refer to the Activity of assigning Tags to things.
Technical Management	(Service Operation) The Function responsible for providing technical skills in support of IT Services and management of the IT Infrastructure. Technical Management defines the Roles of Support Groups, as well as the tools, Processes and Procedures required.
Technical Observation (TO)	(Continual Service Improvement) A technique used in Service Improvement, Problem investigation and Availability Management. Technical support staff meet to monitor the behavior and Performance of an IT Service and make recommendations for improvement.
Technical Service	Synonym for Infrastructure Service.
Technical Support	Synonym for Technical Management.
Tension Metrics	(Continual Service Improvement) A set of related Metrics, in which improvements to one Metric have a negative effect on another. Tension Metrics are designed to ensure that an appropriate balance is achieved.
Terms of Reference (TOR)	(Service Design) A Document specifying the Requirements, Scope, Deliverables, Resources and schedule for a Project or Activity.
Test	(Service Transition) An Activity that verifies that a Configuration Item, IT Service, Process, etc. meets its Specification or agreed Requirements. See Service Validation and Testing, Acceptance.
Test Environment	(Service Transition) A controlled Environment used to Test Configuration Items, Builds, IT Services, Processes etc.

Third Party	A person, group, or Business who is not part of the Service Level Agreement for an IT Service, but is required to ensure successful delivery of that IT Service. For example a software Supplier, a hardware maintenance company, or a facilities department. Requirements for Third Parties are typically specified in Underpinning Contracts or Operational Level Agreements.
Third-line Support	(Service Operation) The third level in a hierarchy of Support Groups involved in the resolution of Incidents and investigation of Problems. Each level contains more specialist skills, or has more time or other Resources.
Threat	Anything that might exploit a Vulnerability. Any potential cause of an Incident can be considered to be a Threat. For example a fire is a Threat that could exploit the Vulnerability of flammable floor coverings. This term is commonly used in Information Security Management and IT Service Continuity Management, but also applies to other areas such as Problem and Availability Management.
Threshold	The value of a Metric which should cause an Alert to be generated, or management action to be taken. For example "Priority1 Incident not solved within 4 hours", "more than 5 soft disk errors in an hour", or "more than 10 failed changes in a month".
Throughput	(Service Design) A measure of the number of Transactions, or other Operations, performed in a fixed time. For example 5000 emails sent per hour, or 200 disk I/Os per second.
Total Cost of Ownership (TCO)	(Service Strategy) A methodology used to help make investment decisions. TCO assesses the full Lifecycle Cost of owning a Configuration Item, not just the initial Cost or purchase price. See Total Cost of Utilization.
Total Cost of Utilization (TCU)	(Service Strategy) A methodology used to help make investment and Service Sourcing decisions. TCU assesses the full Lifecycle Cost to the Customer of using an IT Service. See Total Cost of Ownership.
Total Quality Management (TQM)	(Continual Service Improvement) A methodology for managing continual Improvement by using a Quality Management System. TQM establishes a Culture involving all people in the Organization in a Process of continual monitoring and improvement.
Transaction	A discrete Function performed by an IT Service. For example transferring money from one bank account to another. A single Transaction may involve numerous additions, deletions and modifications of data. Either all of these complete successfully or none of them is carried out.
Transition	(Service Transition) A change in state, corresponding to a movement of an IT Service or other Configuration Item from one Lifecycle status to the next.

Transition Planning and Support	(Service Transition) The Process responsible for Planning all Service Transition Processes and co-coordinating the resources that they require. These Service Transition Processes are Change Management, Service Asset and Configuration Management, Release and Deployment Management, Service Validation and Testing, Evaluation, and Knowledge Management.
Trend Analysis	(Continual Service Improvement) Analysis of data to identify time related patterns. Trend Analysis is used in Problem Management to identify common Failures or fragile Configuration Items, and in Capacity Management as a Modeling tool to predict future behavior. It is also used as a management tool for identifying deficiencies in IT Service Management Processes.
Tuning	The Activity responsible for Planning Changes to make the most efficient use of Resources. Tuning is part of Performance Management, which also includes Performance Monitoring and implementation of the required Changes.
Type I Service Provider	(Service Strategy) An Internal Service Provider that is embedded within a Business Unit. There may be several Type I Service Providers within an Organization.
Type II Service Provider	(Service Strategy) An Internal Service Provider that provides shared IT Services to more than one Business Unit.
Type III Service Provider	(Service Strategy) A Service Provider that provides IT Services to External Customers.
Underpinning Contract (UC)	(Service Design) A Contract between an IT Service Provider and a Third Party. The Third Party provides goods or Services that support delivery of an IT Service to a Customer. The Underpinning Contract defines targets and responsibilities that are required to meet agreed Service Level Targets in an SLA.
Unit Cost	(Service Strategy) The Cost to the IT Service Provider of providing a single Component of an IT Service. For example the Cost of a single desktop PC, or of a single Transaction.
Urgency	(Service Transition) (Service Design) A measure of how long it will be until an Incident, Problem or Change has a significant Impact on the Business. For example a high Impact Incident may have low Urgency, if the Impact will not affect the Business until the end of the financial year. Impact and Urgency are used to assign Priority.
Usability	(Service Design) The ease with which an Application, product, or IT Service can be used. Usability Requirements are often included in a Statement of Requirements.
Use Case	(Service Design) A technique used to define required functionality and Objectives, and to Design Tests. Use Cases define realistic scenarios that describe interactions between Users and an IT Service or other System. See Change Case.
User	A person who uses the IT Service on a day-to-day basis. Users are distinct from Customers, as some Customers do not use the IT Service directly.

User Profile (UP)	(Service Strategy) A pattern of User demand for IT Services. Each User Profile includes one or more Patterns of Business Activity.
Utility	(Service Strategy) Functionality offered by a Product or Service to meet a particular need. Utility is often summarized as "what it does". See Service Utility.
Validation	(Service Transition) An Activity that ensures a new or changed IT Service, Process, Plan, or other Deliverable meets the needs of the Business. Validation ensures that Business Requirements are met even though these may have changed since the original Design. See Verification, Acceptance, Qualification, Service Validation and Testing.
Value Chain	(Service Strategy) A sequence of Processes that creates a product or Service that is of value to a Customer. Each step of the sequence builds on the previous steps and contributes to the overall product or Service. See Value Network.
Value for Money	An informal measure of Cost Effectiveness. Value for Money is often based on a comparison with the Cost of alternatives. See Cost Benefit Analysis.
Value Network	(Service Strategy) A complex set of Relationships between two or more groups or organizations. Value is generated through exchange of knowledge, information, goods or Services. See Value Chain, Partnership.
Value on Investment (VOI)	(Continual Service Improvement) A measurement of the expected benefit of an investment. VOI considers both financial and intangible benefits. See Return on Investment.
Variable Cost	(Service Strategy) A Cost that depends on how much the IT Service is used, how many products are produced, the number and type of Users, or something else that cannot be fixed in advance. See Variable Cost Dynamics.
Variable Cost Dynamics	(Service Strategy) A technique used to understand how overall Costs are impacted by the many complex variable elements that contribute to the provision of IT Services.
Variance	The difference between a planned value and the actual measured value. Commonly used in Financial Management, Capacity Management and Service Level Management, but could apply in any area where Plans are in place.
Verification	(Service Transition) An Activity that ensures a new or changed IT Service, Process, Plan, or other Deliverable is complete, accurate, Reliable and matches its Design Specification. See Validation, Acceptance, Service Validation and Testing.

Verification and Audit	(Service Transition) The Activities responsible for ensuring that information in the CMDB is accurate and that all Configuration Items have been identified and recorded in the CMDB. Verification includes routine checks that are part of other Processes. For example, verifying the serial number of a desktop PC when a User logs an Incident. Audit is a periodic, formal check.
Version	(Service Transition) A Version is used to identify a specific Baseline of a Configuration Item. Versions typically use a naming convention that enables the sequence or date of each Baseline to be identified. For example Payroll Application Version 3 contains updated functionality from Version 2.
Vision	A description of what the Organization intends to become in the future. A Vision is created by senior management and is used to help influence Culture and Strategic Planning.
Vital Business Function (VBF)	(Service Design) A Function of a Business Process which is critical to the success of the Business. Vital Business Functions are an important consideration of Business Continuity Management, IT Service Continuity Management and Availability Management.
Vulnerability	A weakness that could be exploited by a Threat. For example an open firewall port, a password that is never changed, or a flammable carpet. A missing Control is also considered to be a Vulnerability.
Warm Standby	Synonym for Intermediate Recovery.
Warranty	(Service Strategy) A promise or guarantee that a product or Service will meet its agreed Requirements. See Service Validation and Testing, Service Warranty.
Work in Progress (WIP)	A Status that means Activities have started but are not yet complete. It is commonly used as a Status for Incidents, Problems, Changes etc.
Work Instruction	A Document containing detailed instructions that specify exactly what steps to follow to carry out an Activity. A Work Instruction contains much more detail than a Procedure and is only created if very detailed instructions are needed.
Workaround	(Service Operation) Reducing or eliminating the Impact of an Incident or Problem for which a full Resolution is not yet available. For example by restarting a failed Configuration Item. Workarounds for Problems are documented in Known Error Records. Workarounds for Incidents that do not have associated Problem Records are documented in the Incident Record.
Workload	The Resources required to deliver an identifiable part of an IT Service. Workloads may be Categorized by Users, groups of Users, or Functions within the IT Service. This is used to assist in analyzing and managing the Capacity, Performance and Utilization of Configuration Items and IT Services. The term Workload is sometimes used as a synonym for Throughput.

References

Bon, J. van (ed.) (2007). *Foundations of IT Service Management - based on ITIL V3*. Zaltbommel: Van Haren Publishing

Office of Government Commerce (2007). *ITIL: Service Operation*. London: The Stationary Office

Office of Government Commerce (2007). *Glossary ITIL Version 3*: http://www.best-management-practice.com

Index

ITIL Books
The Official Books from itSMF

Foundations of IT Service Management Based on ITIL®V3
Now updated to encompass all of the implications of the V3 refresh of ITIL, the new V3 Foundations book looks at Best Practices, focusing on the Lifecycle approach, and covering the ITIL Service Lifecycle, processes and functions for Service Strategy, Service Design, Service Operation, Service Transition and Continual Service Improvement.
ISBN: 978 908753057 0 (ENGLISH EDITION)
PRICE €39.95 EXCL TAX

Foundations of IT Service Management Based on ITIL®
The bestselling ITIL® V2 edition of this popular guide is available as usual, with 13 language options to give you the widest possible global perspective on this important subject.
ISBN: 978 907721258 5 (ENGLISH EDITION)
PRICE €39.95 EXCL TAX

IT Service Management Based on ITIL®V3: A Pocket Guide
A concise summary for ITIL®V3, providing a quick and portable reference tool to this leading set of best practices for IT Service Management.
ISBN: 978 908753102 7 (ENGLISH EDITION)
PRICE €14.95 EXCL TAX

Van Haren Publishing (VHP) is a leading international publisher, specializing in best practice titles for iT management and business management. VHP publishes in 14 languages, and has sales and distribution agents in over 40 countries worldwide: www.vanharen.net

Other leading ITSM Books from itSMF

Metrics for IT Service Management

A general guide to the use of metrics as a mechanism to control and steer IT service organizations, with consideration of the design and implementation of metrics in service organizations using industry standard frameworks.

ISBN: 978 907721269 1
PRICE €39.95 EXCL TAX

Six Sigma for IT Management

The first book to provide a coherent view and guidance for using the Six Sigma approach successfully in IT Service Management, whilst aiming to merge both Six Sigma and ITIL® into a single unified approach to continuous improvement. Six Sigma for IT Management: A Pocket Guide is also available.

ISBN: 978 907721230 1 (ENGLISH EDITION)
PRICE €39.95 EXCL TAX

Frameworks for IT Management

An unparalleled guide to the myriad of IT management instruments currently available to IT and business managers. Frameworks for IT Management: A Pocket Guide is also available.

ISBN: 978 907721290 5 (ENGLISH EDITION)
PRICE €39.95 EXCL TAX

IT Governance based on CobiT 4.1: A Management Guide

Detailed information on the overall process model as well as the theory behind it.

ISBN: 978 90 8753116 4 (ENGLISH EDITION)
PRICE €20,75 EXCL TAX

Contact your local chapter for ITSM Library titles ...please see www.itsmfbooks.com for details.